Winning Spread Betting Strategies

How to make money in the medium term in up,
down and sideways markets

by Malcolm Pryor

HARRIMAN HOUSE LTD

3A Penns Road
Petersfield
Hampshire
GU32 2EW
GREAT BRITAIN

Tel: +44 (0)1730 233870
Fax: +44 (0)1730 233880
Email: enquiries@harriman-house.com
Website: www.harriman-house.com

First published in Great Britain in 2009 by Harriman House.

978-1-906659-10-3

British Library Cataloguing in Publication Data
A CIP catalogue record for this book can be obtained from the British Library.

For Karen

Contents

About the author

Malcolm Pryor is an active spread bettor and investor, a trading coach, and the author of the best selling book *The Financial Spread Betting Handbook*.

He comments regularly on spread betting issues and on the markets at www.spreadbettingcentral.co.uk. He also runs seminars on spread betting (details at www.sparkdales.co.uk).

He is a member of the Society of Technical Analysts in the UK and has been designated a Certified Financial Technician by the International Federation of Technical Analysts.

He is an expert at several games, including bridge where he has held the rank of Grandmaster or higher for over a decade.

Preface

What this book covers

This book is about using spread betting in a structured way to take advantage of price moves lasting from around a couple of weeks up to several months. Because many people think spread betting is much shorter term than this, the book introduces the *spread betting investor* – a concept used to describe the characteristics of someone using spread betting in this way.

After this concept has been explored in some depth the major part of the book is the detailed description of seven spread betting strategies specifically designed for this duration and matched to whether the market is rising, falling or trading sideways.

Who this book is for

This book is mainly for traders who already use spread betting products and who are looking to develop additional strategies with a very disciplined approach. It is assumed that the reader will already have some familiarity with a range of key trading concepts.

This book may also be of potential interest to those who have not yet got a spread betting account but have heard about spread betting and are keen to see some of the things that can be done with it.

CFDs

This book will also be of potential interest to users of other leveraged derivative products, in particular CFDs. If you trade CFDs, rather than spread betting, just substitute CFD every time you see reference to spread betting. All the strategies in this book can be used with CFDs as the vehicle rather than spread bets.

Key trading concepts

The strategies in this book make use of a range of key trading concepts including:

- getting trading ideas from charts

- going short as well as long

- trading currencies, commodities and indices as well as stocks

- pre-determining exit points before a trade is taken

- limiting risk per trade to a percentage of trading capital.

If these concepts, or others used in this book, are relatively new to you and you want to get a better understanding of them here are some information sources:

1. my first book, *The Financial Spread Betting Handbook*, covers all the basic concepts of spread betting,

2. the website www.spreadbettingcentral.com (there is a forum facility where you can ask questions),

3. I include a list of recommended books in the section of this book called Acquiring skills, and

4. there are some very brief notes in the Appendix.

Investors, traders and spread bettors

Some people think that investors are very different animals from traders. But for me the differences are primarily in the time frames they work in – with investors generally working in longer time frames than traders.

In other respects they are very similar and require similar skills to be successful. Part of the rationale for this book is that spread betting can be used as a vehicle for trading *and* for investing. As such, I use the terms *investor, trader* and *spread bettor* fairly interchangeably in the text of this book

How the book is structured

Part One

The book's first part starts by illustrating the very different results obtained by three stock market investors, depending on the actions they take during bear markets. This leads on to an introduction of the concept of the *spread betting investor*, together with a brief outline of the profile objectives and resources of such an investor.

The following chapter discusses rules of investing and highlights the seven key rules which really separate the winners from losers. Part One concludes with an explanation of the mind-set of the *spread betting investor*.

Part Two

Part Two is the main body of the book. It illustrates the thinking behind, and the steps required to build, successful strategies for three main types of market: up markets, down markets and sideways markets. The strategies are not designed to be followed step-by-step without question – rather they are intended to demonstrate the art of the possible.

The examples contain both winning and losing trades. These are selected to illustrate the implementation stage following the strategy design, and to bring out a number of important points related to the psychology of trading. The examples are not intended to be representative of the results likely to be obtained if the strategies were followed verbatim. Each strategy is formed out of various building blocks which in real life need to be matched to the preferences, objectives and beliefs of the individual.

The seven strategies in Part Two are:

1. buying dips (*market: up*)

2. buying relative strength (*market: up*)

3. selling rallies (*market: down*)

4. selling relative weakness (*market: down*)

5. buying support and selling resistance (*market: sideways*)

6. long/short portfolio (*market: sideways*)

7. early bird (*market: up, down or sideways*)

After an introductory chapter containing a description of various technical analysis tools used in constructing the strategies, each chapter in Part Two contains one of the seven strategies, and each of these chapters has a similar structure:

First the **strategy is introduced,** then in turn we look at:

- **the methodology** of the strategy,
- its **advantages and disadvantages,**
- the **technical challenges** and
- the **solutions to the technical challenges;**

Then we look at **three detailed examples** of the strategy, with each decision point during the life of the example illustrated with charts and commentary.

Supporting website

Further information on all the topics mentioned in this book can be found at the accompanying website: www.spreadbettingcentral.co.uk.

About the charts used in the book

In this book all charts have been produced using ShareScope software (www.sharescope.co.uk).

Acknowledgements

I have many people to thank for providing support, advice and encouragement while writing this book. I shall not be able to name them all personally – but many thanks everyone!

I would like to thank Harriman House for their help in publishing this book, a really great team. In particular, Stephen Eckett, who provides unique editorial wisdom with a light touch.

I would like to take this opportunity of thanking Martin Stamp, the creator of the ShareScope software, and the entire ShareScope team, both for creating the software and for allowing me to reproduce charts from it in this book.

I would like to thank Dr Van Tharp, friend and mentor.

I would like to thank my parents, Maurice, who passed away in 2008, and Marjorie.

And most of all I would like to thank Karen, to whom this book is dedicated.

Risk warning

No responsibility for loss incurred by any person or corporate body acting or refraining to act as a result of reading material in this book can be accepted by the Publisher or the Author.

The information provided by the Author is not offered as, nor should it be inferred to be, advice or recommendation to readers, since the financial circumstances of readers will vary greatly and investment or trading behaviour which may be appropriate for one reader is unlikely to be appropriate for others.

Introduction

There are two common misunderstandings about spread betting, one being that it is just gambling, the other that is just for the short term.

It is easy to see how the gambling misunderstanding comes about. The word "betting" conjures up images of the casino or the race track. The reality is that spread betting is a leveraged derivative product that can form an important part of a trader's arsenal – particularly for those that are successful enough with it to profit more than the capital gains threshold (under current tax laws capital gains tax is not applicable to spread betting). There are of course those that treat spread betting in much the same way as a trip to the casino or the race track with, for the most part, similar results – but this book is not for them.

The view of spread betting being short term is prevalent even amongst experienced practitioners, and it is true that there is a large group of traders who use spread betting for intraday bets, or bets that last just one or two days. But there are others who use spread betting for medium-term trades lasting weeks. This book has been written to illustrate how winning spread betting strategies can be constructed to take such medium-term trades. So, for the most part this book uses weekly charts rather than daily or intraday charts.

There is one other potential misunderstanding which I want to deal with up front. None of the strategies in this book are intended to be followed precisely. All strategies need adapting to the prevailing market and the character of the trader. The intention of this book would be fulfilled if traders took the strategies and adapted them to match their personal objectives and preferences.

Part One
The Spread Betting Investor

A Tale of Three Investors

In this first chapter we look at the fate of three investors, all of whom spent a decade investing in the UK stock market.

For simplicity we will make the assumption that the investments tracked the FTSE All Share Index, and that there were no transaction costs. All three started on 19 October 1998 with £20k, and all three finished on 17 October 2008.

Investor #1: buy and hold

Our first investor reckoned stocks were for the long term. The strategy adopted was simplicity itself. Buy on day one, and hold for the duration. Here is a chart showing how this turned out. The arrows on the chart show the buy and sell points.

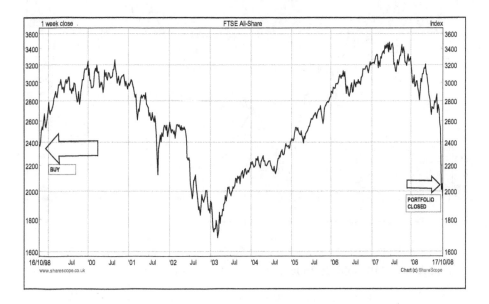

- Bought at 2348, sold at 2051, total decline over the decade 13%, ending capital £17.5k.

And that's with no charges!

Investor #2: sitting out the down-trends

Our second investor had a strong dislike of down-trends. When a down-trend started the technique was to sell everything and wait for a new up-trend. The key question here is how to define when a new down-trend or up-trend has started?

This investor didn't catch the turning points exactly, but overall managed to avoid the worst of the two main down-trends which occurred in the period. The arrows on the chart show the buy and sell points.

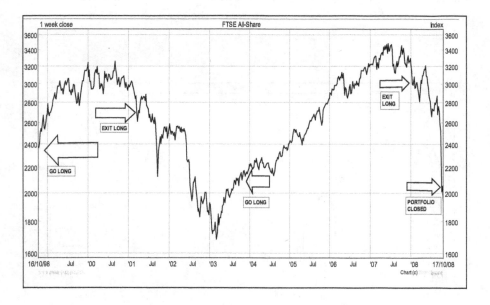

- Bought at 2348, sold at 2696, gain 15%, ending capital £23.0k.

- Then bought at 2095, sold at 3003, gain 43%, ending capital £32.9k.

- Overall increase in capital 65%.

That excludes costs, but also any interest earned while in cash waiting patiently for the down-trends to end.

Investor #3: capitalising on up and down-trends

Our third investor liked down-trends just as much as up-trends – going short in down-trends, and going long in up-trends.

This investor had exactly the same timing as the second investor, but also went short as soon as a down-trend was diagnosed, and as result always had either a long or a short position for the whole decade. The arrows on the chart show the timing for this.

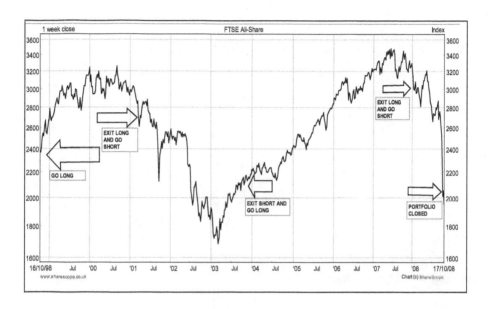

- Went long at 2348, exited long at 2696, gain 15%, ending capital £23.0k.

- Went short at 2696, exited short at 2095, gain 22%, ending capital £28.1k.

- Went long at 2095, exited long at 3003, gain 43%, ending capital £40.3k.

- Went short at 3003, portfolio closed at 2051, gain 32%, ending capital £53.0k.

- Overall increase in capital 165%.

So in summary our first investor bought and hold and lost 13% over the decade. Our investor who sat out the down-trends made 65%. And our investor who rode the up and the down-trends made 165%.

Some cynics may say that it is always easy to pick entry and exit points with hindsight! However, I would emphasise that in the above the investors are not picking the tops and bottoms – just riding the major established (up and down) trends. The purpose of this book is to show that appropriate entry and exit points *can* be determined at the time. In other words, that it *is* possible to time the markets.

Time to introduce the *spread betting investor...*

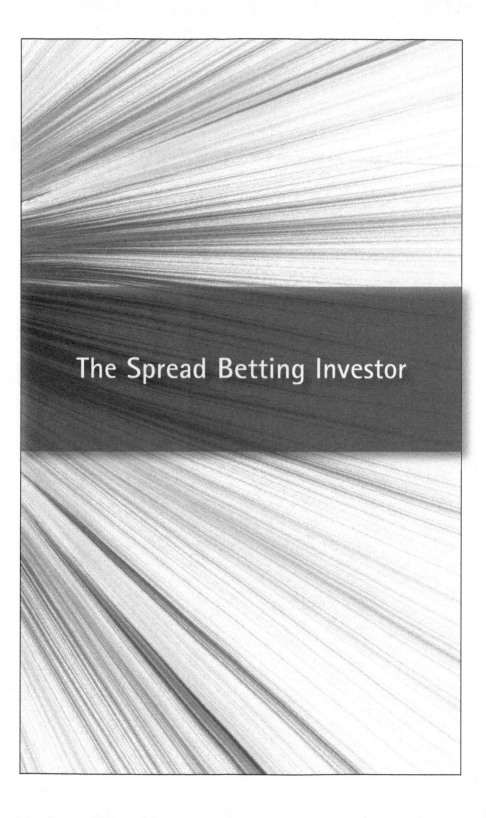

The Spread Betting Investor

Definition

The *spread betting investor* is someone who uses spread betting to take trades that last from several weeks to several months.

Profile

In this book our *spread betting investor* has speculative funds of £20,000, and

1. Actively manages **risk** so that on any one position only 1% (i.e. £200) of those funds can be lost.

2. Long positions are taken when the market is going up, short positions when the market is going down. The *spread betting investor* has **no built in biases for any one direction.**

3. A range of **asset classes** are followed, including stocks, indices and the major currency pairs.

4. **Time** available for analysing the markets is limited, and most trading decisions are made at the weekend, looking at weekly charts.

5. Most **entries and exits** are made either via stop orders or at the open on Monday morning.

Objectives

Objectives for each and every trade are:

1. to **limit risk** to 1% of speculative funds, and

2. to only take trades which present an **attractive ratio of reward-to-risk.**

The strategies chosen to fulfil these objectives also have to be capable of being implemented by busy people with limited available time for market analysis.

Resources

The two main required resources are:

1. a **spread betting account,** ideally one which offers a full range of order types, including market, limit and stop orders

2. **investment software** which facilitates appropriate market analysis (such as the ShareScope software used to create the charts in this book).

The Rules

Some investors' approaches to investing are fairly random; they graze in the field of listed stocks, taking nibbles of stocks that take their fancy. In a bull market this may work out fine (if one always goes long). But to make money in all market conditions one needs a disciplined methodology. This will usually take the form of a set of rules.

The spread betting investor is unlikely to find a simple set of rules that cover every situation. There are, however, common characteristics in the way winners approach investing and we can start to codify some of these into rules.

About rules

Investing is one of the most interesting games anyone could hope to play. And, like most games, there are rules. However, unlike many games, you have to find them out for yourself as you go along.

Who makes up the rules?

In the end, the winning investor makes up their own rules and then plays the game consistently in line with those rules. The losing investor tends to accept incorrect rules given to them by other people.

Who wins, who loses?

The player that wins the investing game is the one that has rules that in the long run lead to success. In poker terms, these rules help them decide which hands to bet on and which ones to fold on.

Some of the players

Let us continue to compare investing using spread bets to playing poker.

In poker, the quality of the opposition potentially affects your results. Here are quotes from some of your opponents in the investing game. If they continue to make these mistakes, and you can avoid these mistakes yourself, you start a little ahead of the game!

"I have to be fully invested all the time."

Says who? Many unit trusts and similar funds have a long only mandate and have to be close to fully invested all the time. But retail investors have a fantastic edge. They can sit out a hand, in other words, they don't have to be fully invested in a bear market. In fact they can go short through various products, and take advantage of the down moves.

"I want all my investing decisions to be winners."

This is not how the game is won. Many top investors win less than 50% of the time, but their winners are a lot bigger than their losers. For these players, that is how they win in the long run.

"Going short is dangerous."

So is going long if you don't manage risk. The issue is not which direction to bet, but the implementation of appropriate risk control procedures.

"I don't use stops."

One of the few certainties in the game is that if you use leverage with no stops you will lose. Do not even think of spread betting unless you are prepared to use stops and manage risk.

"I love the thrill of spread betting."

People who use spread betting as a vehicle for excitement or fun tend to lose most if not all (or more) of their speculative funds. Get your excitement or fun somewhere else, treat investment as business not pleasure.

"I am a discretionary investor."

Some really top investors use discretionary (as opposed to system-based) techniques based on years of high quality experience. However, everyone else needs a rigorous methodology and detailed plans to be successful, and then needs to be able to follow the rules of the methodology with discipline.

As I said, with people in the market thinking the above, if you can employ a sensible disciplined approach to investing it will go a long way towards giving you an edge.

Your move...

In today's world retail investors are able to take advantage of down markets as well as up markets. But to be successful requires having various rules, and following them.

7 investing rules that really count

I list below the seven rules that I believe separate the winners from the losers.

1. Find an edge which works for you

An edge is a predetermined methodology for entering and exiting trades which in the long run can be expected to be profitable. All winners have an edge which is appropriate for them. If you don't know what your edge is you most probably haven't got one. The strategies in this book are designed to help point the way to the process of building a system which has an edge – they are designed to illustrate the process and the thinking behind them, rather than offering off the shelf solutions to be followed verbatim.

2. Assess overall market conditions

This sounds obvious perhaps, but if general market conditions are bullish the focus should be primarily on long trades, if market conditions are bearish the focus should be primarily on short trades, and if market conditions are in sideways mode some mixture of longs and shorts may be appropriate. Ignoring this principle is of course the backdrop for many investors' approaches to bear markets in stocks – stay long and hope for the best.

3. Predetermine your maximum loss on an investment

Winners predetermine their maximum loss on any one investment, and keep it to a sensible percentage of their speculative funds. A commonly adopted benchmark is to aim to only lose 1% on any one investment. Some risk less per investment, say 0.5% or 0.25%, some risk a little more. In a famous saying a top American trader compared people who risked as much as 3% per trade to "gunslingers".

4. Predetermine the point where you will know you are wrong

Top investors predetermine before they enter an investment the point where, if the investment goes against them, they will decide they were wrong and exit at a loss. Before you enter an investment you can be objective, and ensure all the calculations are in line with your objectives; whereas once you are in the investment it is possible that emotions may overrule common sense, and some people have a tendency to give current investments too much leeway.

5. Predetermine your minimum profit potential

Based on technical analysis it is possible to form a judgement on the likely minimum move and therefore profit potential if the investment goes in your favour. Winners try to balance this minimum profit potential against the predetermined maximum loss on the investment. One commonly used rule of thumb is to shoot for at least a 2 to 1 ratio of likely minimum profit-to-risk. Some won't take on an investment unless the ratio is considerably higher than that.

6. Predetermine your rules for exiting

The first rule of exiting is: if the investment reaches the point where you have predetermined that you will know you are wrong and will exit at a loss, get out as predetermined. A common and expensive error is to change your mind at this point, and decide not to get out after all. This is partly because people find it hard to admit they are wrong. But winners do get out at this point and look for new opportunities elsewhere.

The other rule of exiting is how to get out if that initial stop loss is not hit. There are a multitude of techniques here, the key is once again to predetermine rules so that the actual exit decision can be taken promptly and without emotion. The techniques include:

- exiting at a predetermined target,

- exiting after a predetermined period of time, or

- trailing a stop, i.e. as the investment goes in your favour moving the stop according to a predetermined algorithm

7. Schedule periodic checks on how you are doing

Top investors build in regular checks on their performance. There are two main things to check:

1. the performance of the investor,

2. the performance of the strategies they have been using.

If there has been a period of underperformance, is this because the investor has made mistakes, is it just a natural and to be expected temporary down turn in the performance of the strategy, or has there been a significant deterioration in the strategy to the extent that the strategy can be deemed no longer to work as originally intended? For the strategies in this book a periodic check should be diarised for every three months, or more frequently.

The Spread Betting Investor
Mind Set

Just knowing many strategies which can be employed in various markets is not enough for success. In this chapter we look briefly at some other factors which are critical for success.

Objectives

The *spread betting investor* recognises that they are unlikely to reach their destination if they don't know where they are going. As a result, they spend a lot of time initially establishing their objectives. Here are ten starter questions to illustrate some of the thinking required:

1. How much money are you prepared to put into speculative investments?

2. Are you prepared to accept that you might lose all of it?

3. How much time and effort are you prepared to put in to developing the requisite skills to invest well?

4. In which time frame do you want to invest?

5. What percentage return are you targeting?

6. What size drawdown are you budgeting for?

7. Is the relationship of return to drawdown realistic?

8. What is your targeted percentage of winners?

9. What is your targeted ratio of average win to average loss?

10. What percentage of speculative investment capital will be risked per trade?

Knowing yourself

There is a famous saying,

> *if you don't know who you really are, the markets are a very expensive way of finding out*

If you have any weak areas in your investment psychology it is odds on that they will come into play. For example, if your stop discipline is weak chances are you will find yourself hanging on to a loser far too long and taking a loss many multiples larger than your original budgeted risk.

Do you have any addictions? If you have ever had any addiction to gambling stay well away from leveraged products such as spread betting. Spread betting is a useful and practical tool in the investor's tool box, but only if you have the right mental disciplines to actively manage risk. Here is a question to probe this area. Have you ever placed a spread bet or put on a trade just for the excitement of it, for the adrenalin rush? If so, you probably have work to do. (One great site to check out is the site of Van Tharp at www.iitm.com.)

Beliefs about the market

The way I use spread betting is based on what I personally believe works in the market. If you don't share the same beliefs you probably won't be able to invest exactly the same way as me. All the strategies in this book are presented in modular form, so if part of the strategy doesn't match your beliefs feel free to modify it. If the whole strategy is alien to your beliefs, fine, don't use it. The strategies are not there to be used without question, they are an attempt to show how one can put together the building blocks of investing into coherent game plans, based on a set of beliefs about how the market works.

Realism

It is a sad fact that more people are overall losers in the trading game than are winners.

This applies to spread betting, CFDs, futures, options or trading stocks. However, many of the losers would not be losers if they spent a realistic amount of time and energy acquiring relevant skills, and set themselves realistic objectives.

Written plans

All the successful traders I have met have plans for how they trade – mostly documented, some extensively so.

On a day-by-day basis they have a game plan for the day, with specific potential entries and exits pre-planned, along with bet size. For the longer term they have an outline of all the systems they use and an expectation of what their systems will generate, in terms of:

- win/loss ratios,
- average win compared with average loss,
- overally profitability,
- drawdown.

They have contingency plans so that they can rehearse how they will cope with various situations, for example extraordinary market movements, loss of internet connection or sudden illness. They have budgets for trading expenses including software, data and seminars, and these budgets are linked to the size of their speculative funds.

Finally, their trading plans are linked to broader plans, not just financial.

Acquiring skills

There are four main routes to acquiring the relevant skills for investment success:

1. self learning in the market (sometimes referred to as the University of Hard Knocks),

2. through books,

3. through seminars and workshops,

4. by observing and copying what someone else who is successful does.

There is of course some element of overlap between all four of these, and I haven't yet met anyone who has been successful without the first one. The fourth is great, obviously. Books and seminars can provide some short cuts, but expect to move at best like a knight in chess: two squares forward and one sideways.

Technical analysis

For me, technical analysis is the foundation for every trade I make. Although I was once trained as an accountant and as a corporate treasurer, and know how to look at balance sheets, I now have a belief which means I no longer go down any of those roads. The belief (which you may or may not share) is that technical analysis is the only analysis I need, and that it ultimately incorporates all relevant fundamental information.

Books

I list below 25 books that I have read and would recommend.

Intermarket analysis

John J. Murphy: *Intermarket Analysis: Profiting from Global Market Relationships* (John Wiley & Sons Inc., 2004)

Technical analysis

John J. Murphy: *The Visual Investor: How to Spot Market Trends* (John Wiley & Sons Inc., 1996).

John J. Murphy: *Technical Analysis of the Financial Markets: A Comprehensive Guide to Trading Methods and Applications* (New York Institute of Finance, 1999)

Introductions to trading

Dr. Alexander Elder: *Trading for a Living: Psychology, Trading Tactics, Money Management* (John Wiley & Sons Inc., 1993)

Dr. Alexander Elder: *Come into my Trading Room: A Complete Guide to Trading* (John Wiley & Sons Inc., 2002)

Developing trading systems

Tushar S. Chande: *Beyond Technical Analysis: How to Develop and Implement a Winning Trading System* (John Wiley & Sons Inc., 2001)

Bruce Babcock Jr.: *The Business One Irwin Guide to Trading Systems* (Business One Irwin, 1989)

Charles Le Beau & David W. Lucas: *Technical Traders Guide to Computer Analysis of the Futures Market* (McGraw-Hill, 1992)

Curtis M. Faith: *Way of the Turtle: The Secret Methods that Turned Ordinary People into Legendary Traders* (McGraw-Hill, 2007)

Trading issues such as position sizing

Van K. Tharp: *Trade Your Way to Financial Freedom (Second Edition): – Searching for the Holy Grail in the market – Discovering what makes a trader a winning trader – Managing reward to risk in your trades* (Lake Lucerne Limited Partnership, 2007)

Van K. Tharp: *Van Tharp's Definite Guide to Position Sizing: How to Evaluate your System and Use Position Sizing to Meet your Objectives* (The International Institute for Trading Mastery, 2008)

Psychology and trading

Mark Douglas: *Trading in the Zone: Master the Market with Confidence, Discipline and a Winning Attitude* (New York Institute of Finance, 2000)

Interviews, autobiographies, biographies

Jack D. Schwager: *Market Wizards: Interviews with Top Traders* (Harper Business, 1989)

Jack D. Schwager: *The New Market Wizards: Conversations with America's Top Traders* (Harper Business, 1992)

Jack D. Schwager: *Stock Market Wizards: Interviews with America's Top Stock Traders* (John Wiley & Sons Inc., 2001)

Nicholas Darvas: *How I Made $2,000,000 in the Stock Market* (Harriman House, 2007)

Edwin Lefevre: *Reminiscences of a Stock Market Operator* (John Wiley and Sons, Inc., 1993, originally published in 1923 by George H. Doran and Company)

Specific techniques

J. Welles Wilder Jr.: *New Concepts in Technical Trading Systems* (Trend Research, 1978)

Steve Nison: *Japanese Candlestick Charting Techniques: A Contemporary Guide to the Ancient Investment Techniques of the Far East* (New York Institute of Finance, 2001)

Steve Nison: *Beyond Candlesticks: New Japanese Charting Techniques Revealed* (John Wiley & Sons Inc., 1994)

John Bollinger: *Bollinger on Bollinger Bands* (McGraw-Hill, 2002)

Jeremy du Plessis: *The Definitive Guide to Point and Figure: A Comprehensive Guide to the Theory and Practical Use of the Point and Figure Charting Method* (Harriman House, 2005)

Richard W Arms, Jr: *Stop and Make Money: How to Profit in the Stock Market Using Volume and Stop Orders* (John Wiley & Sons Inc., 2008)

Set ups

David Landry: *Dave Landry on Swing Trading* (M. Gordon Publishing Group, 2002)

Laurence A. Connors & Linda Bradford Raschke: *Street Smarts: High Probability Short Term Trading Strategies* (M. Gordon Publishing Group, 1995)

Websites

Here are some websites to check out.

www.spreadbettingcentral.co.uk

This is the website I edit. It includes market analysis and regular blogs on a range of spread betting and trading issues. This site also provides links to spread betting firms and to sites providing resources for spread betting.

www.stockcharts.com

A subscription site, but with several useful free areas. In particular the Market Summary in the Free Charts area, and the Chart School, which provides explanations of a range of technical analysis tools.

www.sparkdales.co.uk

Information on training seminars run by the author.

www.iitm.com

This is the site of Dr Van Tharp, psychologist and trading coach, featured in *Market Wizards* (recommended reading).

www.sharescope.co.uk

This is the site of the provider of the software used to produce all the charts in this book.

Training

Training in investing, trading and spread betting falls into three main categories:

1. training provided by brokers and spread betting firms,

2. training provided by software firms featuring primarily their own software

3. training provided by third parties (firms or individuals)

There is a huge range in price and scope. It is always a good idea to do some research before spending money on training; if you can, speak to previous attendees.

Experience

Readers of my first book will recognise here one of my favourite trading quotes.

> *"Despite our constant pursuit of knowledge, the market itself assures there is no shortcut to obtaining our final degree. In the end, it is experience which is our ultimate teacher and there is no substitute. We can only choose the attitude with which we approach this process of learning to trade."*

> *Street Smarts: High Probability Short Term Trading Strategies*, Laurence A. Connors & Linda Bradford Raschke

Winning attitudes

The more traders I meet the more it becomes clear that winners and losers set about the tasks of trading with different attitudes. Here are 10 winning traits, adapted from my previous book, *The Financial Spread Betting Handbook*, summarised into rules.

1. Have written plans and rules

2. Never trade without an edge

3. Only use methods that suit you

4. Understand the rewards, risks and odds of your methods

5. Stay in control of your trading and yourself

6. Focus on planning your exits

7. Don't risk too much on any one trade, or in aggregate

8. Stay in tune with the markets

9. Monitor your performance, and adapt

10. Accept it is down to you and no one else

Part Two

7 Spread Betting Investor Strategies

In Part Two we look at seven different strategies which are categorised according to whether the overall market is going up down or sideways. The strategies are listed in the following table.

Strategy	Overall Market
1. Buying dips	Up
2. Buying relative strength	Up
3. Selling rallies	Down
4. Selling relative weakness	Down
5. Buying support and selling resistance	Sideways
6. Long / short portfolio	Sideways
7. Early bird	Up, Down or Sideways

We will start off by choosing the technical analysis tools to define *up*, *down* and *sideways*, plus a number of other tools required for the various strategies. Then we look at each strategy in turn.

You will see with each strategy that we have technical issues to resolve, and various options are presented to solve those technical issues. The solutions are a matter for individual investor preference, and will depend on style, experience and objectives. The intention here is to demonstrate the art of the possible rather than present strategies to be followed to the letter.

It is worth pointing out up front that a similar structured approach is taken in developing each strategy. As a result each chapter containing one of the seven strategies has a similar look and feel to it. You might feel as you read one of the later chapters that you have "been here before". This is quite deliberate; successful traders are for the most part very methodical in their approach, building structured (written) plans for their trading and then implementing those plans in a disciplined way. If this feels in any way bureaucratic or tedious to anyone and they are looking for something more glamorous this is probably a serious warning sign to do some more work on the psychological aspects of trading before risking money on real life trading.

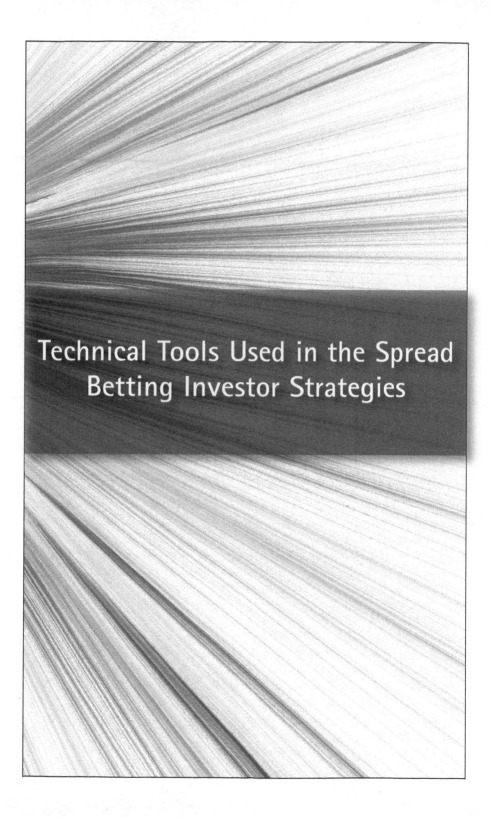

Technical Tools Used in the Spread Betting Investor Strategies

Tools to define up, down and sideways

In this section I first describe in outline the various tools used, then present a number of charts illustrating their use. Note that the descriptions are fairly brief and focus on the use of the tools rather than the mechanics of how they are constructed. (Further details on these tools can be found at www.spreadbettingcentral.co.uk.)

Visual inspection

If you can look at a chart and it is obvious that price has been going up, or obvious that price has been going down or going sideways, then that is probably what the technical analysis tools will also indicate. Bear in mind that most technical analysis tools and indicators are just derivatives of up to five types of data, the open, the high, the low, the close and volume. Visual inspection forms part of our armoury for implementing our strategies.

ADX

ADX (Average Directional Index) is a useful tool which helps to analyse whether or not a trend is in place. The most common setting for the indicator is 14 periods, but I like to use a lower setting. In this book, since we are primarily looking at weekly charts, we will be using an 8 week ADX.

The ADX tool comprises three components:

- **+DI**, shown on the charts as a dotted line, is based on how much price action has taken place above the high of the previous period. The higher the reading the more price action has taken place above the high of the previous period. Logically one would expect higher readings in up-trends and lower readings in down-trends.

- **−DI**, shown on the charts as a dashed line, is based on how much price action has taken place below the low of the previous period. The higher the reading the more price action has taken place below the low of the previous period. Logically one would expect higher readings in down-trends and lower readings in up-trends.

- The **ADX** line itself, shown on the charts as a solid line, is based on the difference between the +DI and the −DI lines.

Interpretations of the ADX tool vary from simple to highly complex. In this book we will using the tool in a fairly simple way. The key interpretations are:

- +DI has a higher reading than –DI: an up-trend

- –DI has a higher reading than +DI: a down-trend

- the two DI lines crisscross each other: a sideways market

- the ADX line rises above 25: a significant up-trend or down-trend

- a rising ADX line above 25: associated with a continuing trend

- a falling ADX line above 25; associated with a trend which is either consolidating or potentially reversing.

Moving average combinations

Moving averages help us to see the wood for the trees. They enable us to bring overall trends into focus, while eliminating the distraction of the inevitable fluctuations around the trends. There are two main types: *exponential* and *simple*. Exponential apply a greater weighting to more recent prices and therefore react more quickly to changes in the direction of prices; but simple moving averages also have many fans. In this book we will use exponential moving averages.

Moving averages can be applied to any time period, and to any price data. We will apply moving averages to weekly closing prices.

There are many thousands of combinations of moving averages possible. We will use the combination of a 4 week, a 10 week and a 40 week moving average. Note that these are roughly equivalent to 20 day, 50 day and 200 day moving averages which are very commonly used to describe the short, intermediate and long-term trend, respectively.

Interpretation of moving averages

There are many popular interpretations of moving averages. For example:

- traders commonly inspect the slope of a moving average to determine the trend in that time frame, up down or sideways

- traders look at the relationship between different moving averages; a shorter one above a longer one is bullish, a shorter one below a longer one is bearish.

We can use moving averages to define markets in the following way:

- *Up-trend, flowing*: 4 week average above the 10 week, 10 week average above the 40 week, all three averages pointing up

- *Up-trend, stalling*: 4 week average above the 10 week, 10 week average above the 40 week, less than three averages pointing up

- *Down-trend, flowing*: 4 week average below the 10 week, 10 week average below the 40 week, all three averages pointing down

- *Down-trend, stalling*: 4 week average below the 10 week, 10 week average below the 40 week, less than three averages pointing down

- *Sideways*: any other layout.

For some strategies a trend stalling will provide an opportunity to get on board the trend, and for other strategies a trend stalling will provide the signal to exit. Some strategies will only be used in sideways markets.

Examples

Here are five charts of different types of market showing how both the ADX tool and the moving average combinations typically behave in each type of market.

Chart 2.1: trend analysis – flowing up-trend

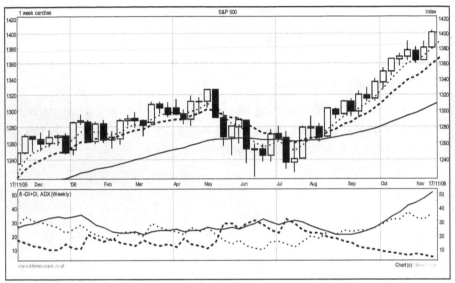

Look at the period from August to the end of the chart, showing a "flowing" up-trend in the S&P 500. The up-trend is obvious to visual inspection. The moving averages are all pointing up, with the 4 week average above the 10 week, and the 10 week one above the 40 week. The ADX line rises above 25 and continues rising, with +DI above –DI.

Chart 2.2: trend analysis – stalled up-trend

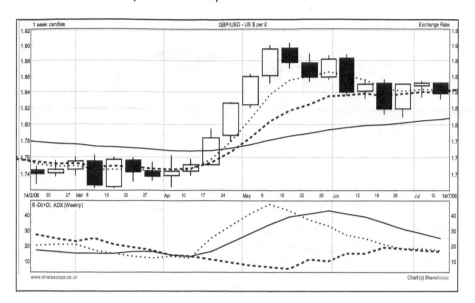

From late April to mid May you will recognise the characteristics of a flowing up-trend which we have just reviewed.

Notice at the end of the chart there is a retracement of the up-trend. After such a powerful move up it is quite normal for there to be a period of consolidation. This is a stalled up-trend. It can be identified through visual inspection, and the technical analysis tools give the same message. The moving averages are still in the order we expect for an up-trend (4 week above 10 week and 10 week above 40 week) but the 4 week has turned down and is approaching the 10 week, and the 10 week has flattened. The ADX line has turned down and has fallen to 25, and although the +DI line is still above the –DI line they are very close to each other.

Chart 2.3: trend analysis – flowing down-trend

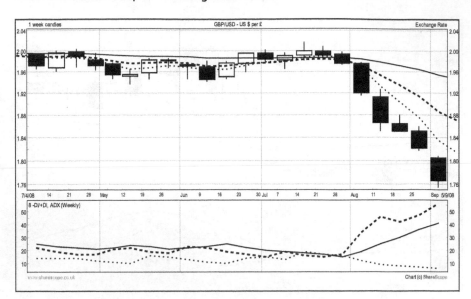

At the end of this chart of Sterling Dollar we have a flowing down-trend – obvious to visual inspection. The moving averages are clearly in down-trend mode, all pointing down, with the 4 week below the 10 week and the 10 week below the 40 week. The ADX line rises above 25 and continues to rise with – DI above +DI.

Chart 2.4: trend analysis – stalled down-trend

For the final few bars at the end of this chart of the General Financial sector we have a stalled down-trend, a period of consolidation identifiable via visual inspection. The 4 week moving average is still below the 10 week and the 10 week below the 40 week but both the 4 week and the 10 week have turned up. The ADX line has been falling and at the end of the chart has reached the 25 level and the +DI is getting close to the –DI line.

Chart 2.5: trend analysis – sideways market

The last few months on this chart of the FTSE 100 show clearly what a sideways market looks like, which is obvious via visual inspection. The slowest moving average, the 40 week average is still pointing slightly down since it still contains data from an earlier down-trend, but the 4 week and 10 week averages go sideways and crisscross each other. The ADX line sinks to levels way below 25 and the +DI and –DI lines crisscross each other.

Tools to define short-term dips and rallies

RSI

RSI (Relative Strength Index) is a popular indicator for assessing whether price is high or low relative to its own past action over a user-defined period. In a sideways market some traders like to sell when this indicator reaches high levels and buy when it reaches low levels. In trending markets this approach is dangerous, since in a strong up-trend the indicator can give high readings for an extended period of time, and in a strong down-trend can give low readings for an extended period of time. In trending markets therefore the indicator is more useful as a tool to help define corrections to the trend, which can be exploited as opportunities to enter the trend.

A high reading is traditionally defined as in the range 70 to 100, a low reading is traditionally defined as 0 to 30. Common settings for the indicator are 14 and 9 periods, however lower settings can also be used, and in this book we use a 3 period RSI.

Chart 2.6: RSI example

This chart of Sterling Dollar is an example of how the RSI indicator behaves in a sideways market, high readings tending to correlate with short-term price peaks, low readings with price troughs.

Weekly highs and lows

The highest price reached in the week has significance, showing the limits of the power of buyers to push prices higher; similarly the lowest price, showing the limits of the power of the sellers to push prices lower. In many of the strategies we use a break of the previous week's high or low as a signal to enter a trade.

Other technical analysis tools

Relative strength

Not to be confused with RSI outlined earlier, relative strength compared price action with the price action of another security. Some of the strategies we use for stocks look for outperformance or underperformance versus either the stock's sector or the overall market.

Support and resistance

Very simply, support is a price level or area where in the past price has stopped going down and turned back up again. Resistance is a price level or area where in the past price has stopped going up and turned back down again. These levels or areas tend to continue to act as barriers to price movement if market participants become aware of them and take action based on them.

Weekly pivots

A weekly pivot low is a weekly bar with two higher lows either side of it. It shows the point where over the three weeks concerned the sellers ran out of power to push prices any lower. A weekly pivot high is a weekly bar with two lower highs either side of it. It shows the point where over the three weeks concerned the buyers ran out of power to push prices any higher. Weekly pivots have significance as support and resistance levels.

Momentum

Momentum measures the rate of increase or decrease in an upward or downward movement. The theory is that changes in momentum precede changes in price direction. The classic analogy is with a ball being thrown up in the air. The rate of increase in the height of the ball starts slowing down before the ball starts falling. Various momentum indicators are available, all with user-defined periods. In this book we use a simple momentum indicator which compares the week's closing price to the closing price 6 weeks earlier, expressed as a percentage.

Divergence

We use the concept of indicator divergence, which is where price behaves in one way and the indicator behaves in another. Various forms of divergence are believed to have predictive value. Specifically with regard to momentum indicators, if price makes a new low but the indicator fails to make a new low, this can be interpreted as a sign that the down-trend may be about to end.

Trading concepts

Stops

The use of stops is integral to all the strategies. Predetermining a point at which the trade will be exited if it goes against us serves two critical purposes:

1. we predetermine the maximum loss we are prepared to incur on a given trade,

2. we provide a benchmark against which to measure the actual profit or loss incurred on the trade.

Cost of carry

Profit and loss figures for the various trades illustrated in the examples do not include cost of carry which will potentially reduce profit on long trades and add to profit on short trades.

Pyramiding

Although pyramiding is not used in any of the examples in this book, some readers may find some use for it as they develop their approach to some of the strategies.

Pyramiding is a simple concept, but complex in its execution. The basic principle of pyramiding is adding to existing winning positions with the objective of increasing the total gain. The technical issues are:

1. when to add to the position

2. how much to add to the position

3. where to move stops to

A very simple scheme on a short sale might be to sell 4 units initially, then add a further 2 units after price has moved the same distance as the distance from entry to initial stop, at the same time moving the stop to the original entry level. This way, the first 4 units will do no worse than breakeven, and the risk on the second 2 units will equate to half the initial risk.

Two generally accepted principles of pyramiding are:

1. never add to a losing position,

2. make additions to the position on a smaller scale than the initial position.

Important note on the strategy examples

The examples have been selected to illustrate the strategies. They are not intended to be a representative sample of the results of operating the strategies. In particular, although a number of losing trades have been illustrated, the examples do not include a representative number of losing trades for the various strategies shown.

Strategy 1 – Buying Dips

Introduction to the strategy

This strategy is applicable to all asset classes. For stocks it is most effective when the overall market is clearly in bull mode, or when particular market sectors are clearly in bull mode. It also works well with other asset classes when the up-trend stands out. It enters positions after the trend has already formed, and it tends to get out before the trend is over; in other words, it aims to get a piece of the action while controlling risk, rather than capturing the whole trend.

Strategy methodology

The basic methodology of this strategy when applied to stocks is:

1. overall market is going up

2. the stock's sector is going up

3. the stock is going up

4. we wait for a short-term dip in the stock

5. we wait for the short-term dip to end

6. we calculate how much capital to risk on this trade

7. we determine where our protective stop will be

8. we calculate trade size based on 6 and 7

9. then we go long

10. we stay long until we get a signal to get out

Note: There is a slight variation in this strategy for commodities, indices, bonds and currencies, where the strategy starts at Step 3.

Advantages and disadvantages of the strategy

The main advantages of this strategy are:

- We are in accord with the overall direction of the market, the sector and the stock; market conditions are on our side, we are not fighting against them.

- By waiting for a short-term dip we get an improved entry price and can define a logical point for a stop (below the low of the dip).

- Our trade size is a function of how much we are prepared to risk and where our stop will be.

The main disadvantage of this strategy is that not all up-trends we want to take advantage of will provide us with the opportunity to enter after a short-term dip – we are going to miss some.

Technical challenges of the strategy

The main technical challenges in implementing this strategy are:

1. what time frame to trade this strategy on

2. how to define the overall market

3. how to define "going up"

4. how to define a short-term dip

5. how to define when the short-term dip has ended

6. how to determine how much capital to risk

7. how to determine where to put our protective stop

8. how to define the signal to get out

We will now look at answering those questions.

Solutions to the technical challenges of the strategy

1) What time frame to trade this strategy on

We will take trades off weekly charts, and expect trades to last from weeks to months.

2) How to define the overall market

We will use the FTSE All Share Index.

3) How to define "going up"

- Visual inspection, or

- ADX, or

- moving average combinations.

4) How to define a short-term dip

- 3 week RSI oversold, or

- a weekly low lower than at least the previous 2 weekly lows.

5) How to define when the short-term dip has ended

We will adopt the solution that it has ended when price rises above the previous week's high.

6) How to determine how much capital to risk

For all the examples we will assume we have total speculative funds of £20,000, and we will risk 1% on each trade (i.e. £200).

Note: This is a solution for traders who have mastered all the relevant techniques – less experienced traders should risk less than this (e.g. 0.25% or less).

---

7) How to determine where to put our protective stop

We will place our protective stop immediately below the low of the week of entry and the two previous weeks.

8) How to define the signal to get out

We have already determined that our protective stop is below the low of the last two weeks; if that is hit we will exit. Otherwise we will stay in the trade until either:

- −DI climbs above +DI, suggesting the up-trend is over, or

- at least one of the moving averages turns down, suggesting the up-trend is stalling.

Example 1 – Euro Dollar

Here is a chart showing the initial set up point for this trade.

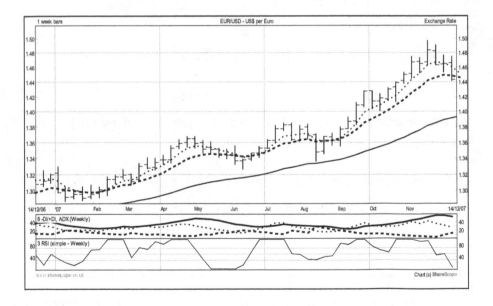

Visual inspection shows that this currency pair (which shows how many Dollars there are to 1 Euro) has been in a strong up-trend. The ADX indicator is over 25 with +DI greater than −DI. The moving averages are in up-trend mode, but stalling (the 4 week average has already turned down, and the 10 week average appears on the verge on turning down). Price has been falling for several weeks, and the 3 week RSI is now below 30 (oversold). If the up-trend reasserts itself by rising above the high of this week, we will go long. Our entry price will be 1.4760, with a stop below the low of the week of entry and the two previous weeks.

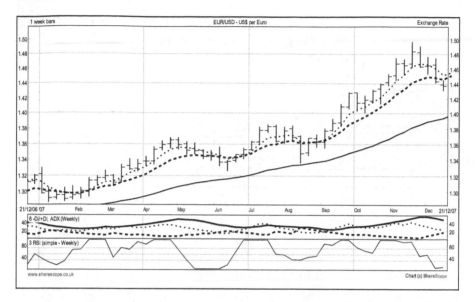

A week on, price has failed to exceed the high of the previous week. Both the ADX indicator and the moving average configuration are in up-trend mode. The 3 week RSI remains oversold, and we will still want to go long if the up-trend reasserts itself by rising above the high of this week. Our new entry price will be 1.4460, with a stop below the low of the week of entry and the two previous weeks.

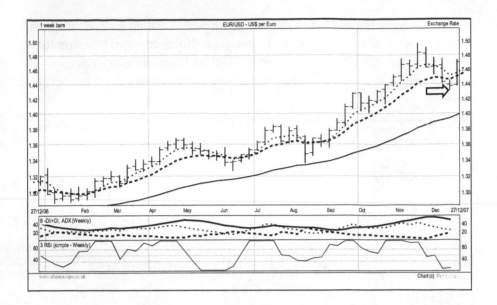

Our trigger for entry was hit this week, as price reached the 1.4460 level. Our protective stop is below the low of the week of entry and the two previous weeks, at 1.4300. (marked by the arrow).

Euro Dollar bets are usually priced in a whole number of pounds per 0.0001 dollars, so we have bet £1 per 0.0001 Dollar, which means our risk on this bet is £160 (1.4460 – 1.4300 divided by 0.0001). £2 per 0.0001 Dollar would have increased our risk to £320, way over our budget of £200 per trade.

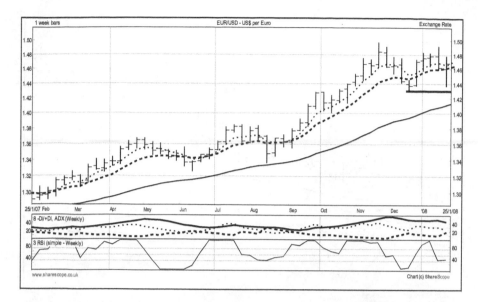

A month into this trade and not much progress. Price went up, then fell back to below our entry level. But our protective stop marked by the thick black line has not been hit, and we have not received any signal to exit, so we will stay with it.

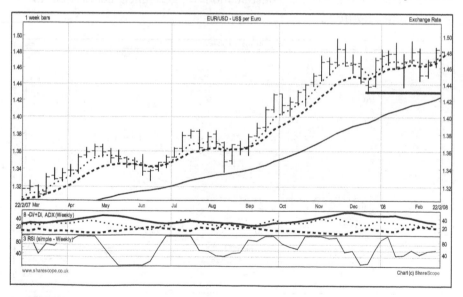

Eight weeks into this trade now, and we have been back close to our entry price a couple more times. Both the 4 week and the 10 week moving average have come close to turning down, but not decisively, and –DI has come close to crossing above +DI; but we have received no clear signal to exit yet. Our risk is still limited by our protective stop, marked by the thick black line. Nothing to do but wait patiently.

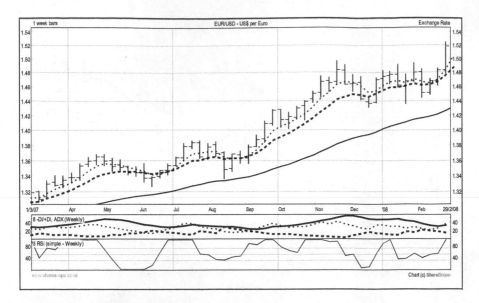

What a difference one week can make!

This is a very promising development for our trade, since price has now broken strongly upwards out of the consolidation range, which bodes well for a renewal of the up-trend.

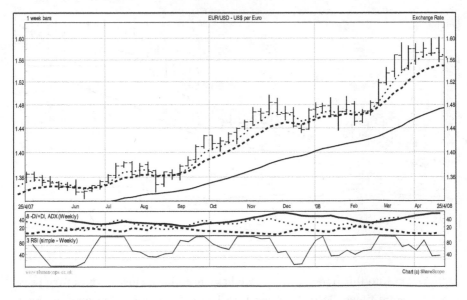

One of our signals to exit is a turn down in one of the moving averages. Here the 4 week and 10 week moving averages both look like they are trying to turn down, but the signal is not quite decisive enough (almost, but not quite). We will give it another week.

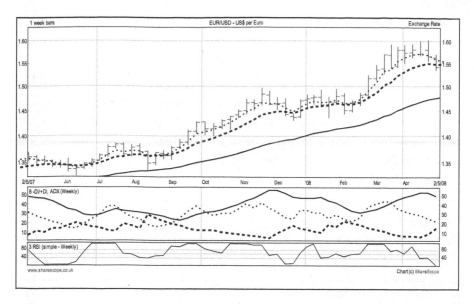

With hindsight it would have been better to have exited a week ago. But it is important to remember that this is an inexact science, full of close calls and trade offs, some of which go our way and some of which don't. It is now obvious that the 4 week moving average has turned down, and that is a clear signal for us to exit this trade as soon as the markets open next week.

Trade summary

Field	Value
Instrument	Euro Dollar
Long / short	Long
Entry	1.4460
£s per point	1
Protective stop	1.4300
Exit	1.5520
Risk (£s)	160 ((1.4460-1.4300) / 0.0001)
Risk as a % of trading capital	0.8
Profit (£s)	1060 ((1.5520 – 1.4460) / 0.0001)
Profit-to-risk ratio	6.6
Percentage move	7.3
Length of trade (weeks)	19

This turned out to be a good trade in the end. The ratio of profit-to-risk of 6.6 is good. A few trades with that kind of ratio more than compensate for the inevitable losers which occur with this strategy.

The trade was interesting from a psychological perspective. It took a couple of months to really get going, and an impatient trader might well have exited it before it got going. We gave up some profits at the end, which is a necessary trade off for potentially enjoying more of the up-trend. This is a psychological hurdle for the inexperienced trader, who will tend to focus more on the "lost profits" rather than the overall success of the trade.

Example 2 – Crude oil

Here is a chart showing the initial set up point for this trade.

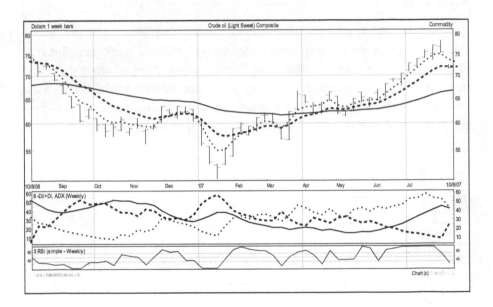

Visual inspection shows a strong up-trend which has taken price from around $50 to around $78. The ADX indicator is well above 25 with +DI above –DI. The moving averages are in up-trend mode, but now stalling. The 3 week RSI has fallen to below 30, oversold, and price has fallen below the low of the previous several weeks. We want to go long of crude oil if the up-trend is renewed. We will go long if price exceeds the high of this week, with a protective stop below the low of the entry week and the previous two weeks.

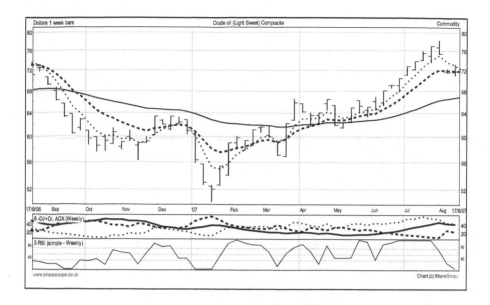

Our entry point for this trade was reached, $72.28. Our protective stop, below the low of the entry week and the two previous weeks, is at $70.92.

Bets on crude oil are priced in whole £s per $0.01, and we have bet £1 per $0.01. Our risk is £136 (72.28 – 70.92 divided by 0.01). £2 per $0.01 would have increased our risk to £272, too high for us given our desire to limit risk to £200 per trade.

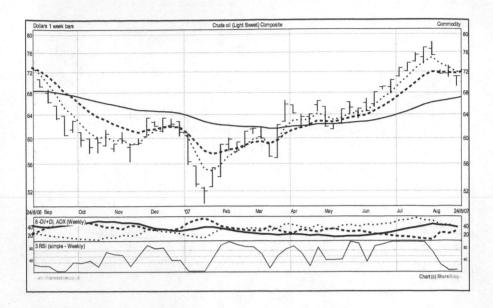

Our protective stop has been hit, so we are out, no questions asked. The best way to guarantee getting out is to automate our stop on the spread betting firm's trading platform, but if we haven't done that we should have seen the signal and acted on it immediately. We are out of the trade. The purpose of the protective stop is to protect our capital when our bets do not work out for us. We just do not know how much further price will fall now it has dropped below the low of this retracement.

Getting out of this crude oil trade now does not mean we cannot get into another crude oil trade later. In fact, we note, after exiting the trade, that our set up conditions to go long still exist. We can watch from the sidelines with no more capital at risk to see if a new entry is triggered.

Trade summary

Field	Value
Instrument	Crude oil
Long / short	Long
Entry	72.28
£s per point	1
Protective stop	70.92
Exit	70.92
Risk (£s)	136 (72.28 – 70.92 divided by 0.01)
Risk as a % of trading capital	0.7
Loss (£s)	136
Loss to risk ratio	1.0
Percentage move	1.9 against us
Length of trade (weeks)	1

One of the secrets of successful trading is to cut losses short and let winners run. A good way of doing this is to make sure our losses are never more than the amount we risked when we entered the trade, and to try to get our winners to be several multiples of that risk. Here we have exited promptly as the trade hits our stop, losing only what we risked at the outset of the trade, and we should therefore regard this as a job well done.

Another interesting point here: all our set up conditions for a new long trade are still valid. Psychologically many traders would find it hard to consider re-entering a trade they had just lost money on. So the question to ask is: would we be considering the trade if we hadn't just lost money on crude oil? In this case the answer is yes, since visual inspection, the ADX indicator and the moving average configuration all indicate an up-trend. The 3 week RSI is way below 30, oversold. A classic set up using this strategy.

As it happens a new long trade was triggered the following week, and we were able to ride a renewed up-trend from around $72 to just above $90.

Example 3 – Lonmin PLC

Here are three charts showing the initial set up point for this trade.

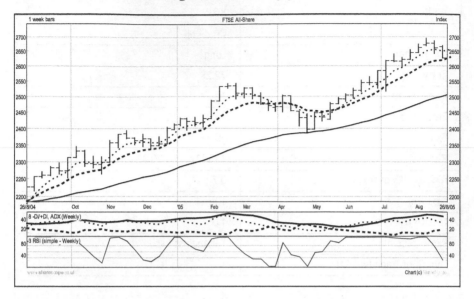

Visual inspection shows that the overall market has been in a strong up-trend. The ADX indicator is well over 25 with +DI higher than –DI. The moving averages are in up-trend mode.

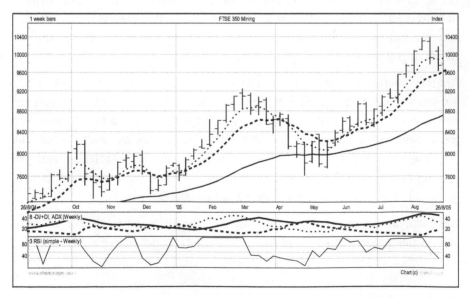

Visual inspection shows that the mining sector has been in a strong up-trend. The ADX indicator is well over 25 with +DI higher than –DI. The moving averages are in up-trend mode.

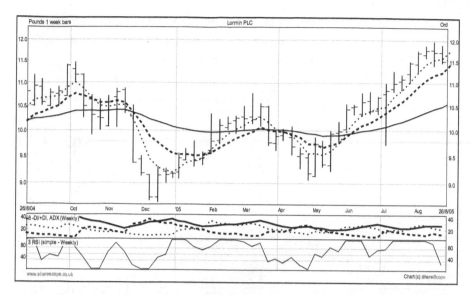

Visual inspection shows that Lonmin has been rising for the last few months. The ADX indicator is only marginally above 25, with +DI higher than –DI, but the moving averages are clearly in up-trend mode. The 3 week RSI has dropped well below 30, the level indicating an oversold status. We would like to go long if price exceeds the high of this week, with a stop below the low of the entry week and the two previous weeks.

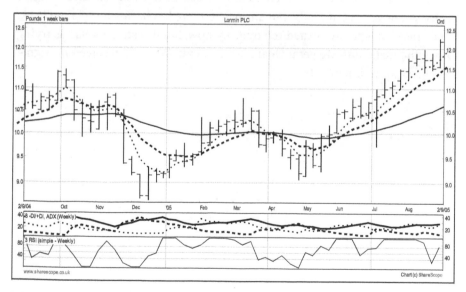

During the week price moved up above last week's high, and we entered this trade at 1189. Our stop was below the low of the entry week and the two previous weeks, at 1138.

Bets in Lonmin are priced in pounds per point (with a point being one penny). We have bet £4 per point. Our risk is £204 (1189 – 1138 times 4), within tolerance levels of our predetermined risk per trade of £200.

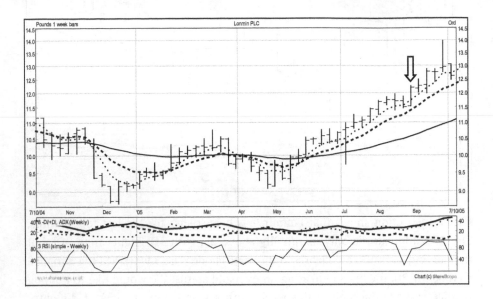

A few weeks on from when we entered the trade (marked by the arrow). Price almost got up to 1400 recently, but since then there has been a bit of a pullback. Some traders might have exited the trade by now, but this strategy has us trying to ride the trend until we get a clear signal to exit. We have received no signal to exit, so we wait patiently.

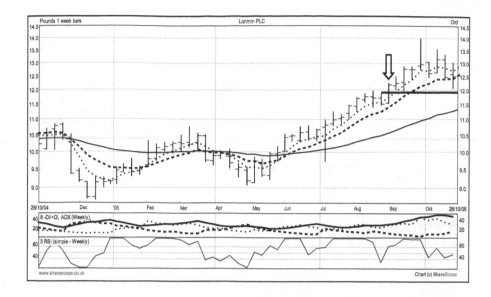

On this chart the week we entered is marked with an arrow, and the price we entered at is marked with a thick horizontal line. We have now been in the trade eight weeks, and it has been a roller coaster ride. At one stage price got nearly to 1400 (at which point we were in profit by about the amount we originally risked), and now this last week price fell back at one point to almost our entry price.

Some traders might find this stressful.

But using this strategy we have still had no signal to exit; although the 4 week moving average has wobbled a bit it has yet to turn down decisively.

What is the worst that can happen now?

We might lose the amount we originally risked; plus we have tied up some capital for a couple of months, and incurred some cost of carry charges. So we will wait patiently in the knowledge that we have a protective stop, and give this strategy some more time to work.

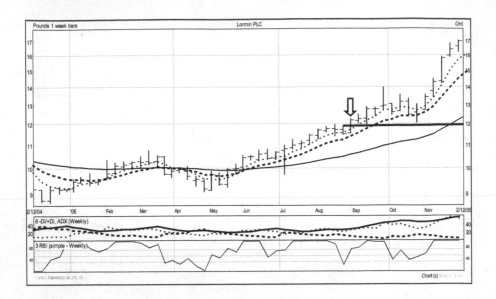

Five weeks later, and the trade has now been progressing well, price first reaching the previous high point near 1400, then surging on upwards. Once again the week we entered is shown with an arrow, the entry price with a thick horizontal line.

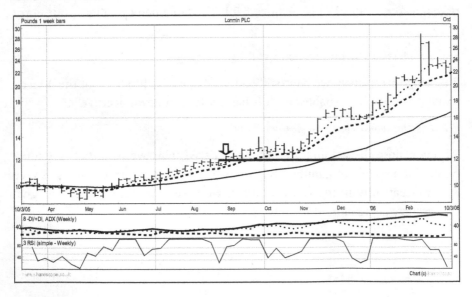

28 weeks into the trade, and it has started to win big time. At its peak price reached 2860, at which point we were in profit to the tune of £6684. The closing price last week was 2259, so we are now £4280 in profit.

This is a potentially stressful situation for many traders, and there are alternative techniques we could use to lock in profits when they reach a certain size. These include selling part of the holding or moving our protective stop closer on part or all of the holding. The technical issues to consider if altering the strategy in this way include:

- What size profits will make us modify our exit methodology?

- How specifically will we modify the exit methodology when those profits have been achieved?

We choose not to make such modifications to our strategy, and accept that sometimes quite significant profits will at least temporarily be given back, and that this is the price we pay for trying to ride the trend as long as we can. In this case, no signal for exit has been given yet, so we stick with the trade.

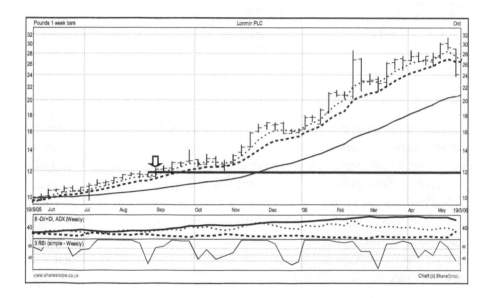

Now finally we have received a signal to exit. The 4 week moving average line has turned down decisively. We will exit as soon as the markets open next week. The chart shows us the whole history of this long trade, the arrow marking the week we entered and the horizontal line the price we entered at.

Trade summary

Field	Value
Instrument	Lonmin
Long / short	Long
Entry	1189
£s per point	4
Protective stop	1138
Exit	2350
Risk (£s)	204
Risk as a % of trading capital	1.0
Profit (£s)	4644
Profit-to-risk ratio	22.8
Percentage move	97.6
Length of trade (weeks)	38

This has been an exceptional trade, with a profit-to-risk ratio of 22.8.

The trade demonstrates some of the psychological difficulties traders have in running winners. Some traders would have ditched the trade at the 8 week stage, after it had appeared not to have got anywhere, and thereby missed out on one of the best trades of the year. Others would have been so keen to bag a profit, any profit, that they would have got out with perhaps £400 or £600 profit. And there will be others that look ruefully at the maximum profit achieved in the life of the trade and compare it unfavourably with the actual profit achieved, perhaps wondering if there is some magic technique that will help them pick the top next time.

Strategy 2 – Buying Relative Strength

Introduction to the strategy

This strategy is for stocks. It is most effective when the market and the stock's sector are both in clear up-trends. It goes long of stocks which are outperforming market and sector, and stays long while the relative strength continues.

Strategy methodology

The basic methodology of this strategy is:

1. overall market is going up

2. the stock's sector is going up

3. the stock is going up

4. the stock is strong relative to the overall market and the sector

5. we calculate how much capital to risk on this trade

6. we determine where our protective stop will be

7. we calculate trade size based on 5 and 6

8. then we go long

9. we stay long until we get a signal to get out

Advantages and disadvantages of the strategy

The main advantages of this strategy are:

1. We are in accord with the overall direction of the market, the sector our stock is in and the stock itself. Market conditions are on our side, we are not fighting against them

2. Our trade size is a function of how much we are prepared to risk and where our stop will be.

3. The strategy can capture significant portions of an established up-trend.

The main disadvantage of this strategy is that while relative strength continues it tends to ride out periods of consolidation and of retracement, rather than exiting; and it will also miss out on continuations of an up-trend when relative strength ceases.

Technical challenges of the strategy

The main technical challenges in implementing this strategy are:

1. what time frame to trade this strategy on

2. how to define the overall market

3. how to define "going up"

4. how to define relative strength versus the overall market

5. how to define relative strength versus the sector

6. how to determine how much capital to risk

7. how to determine where to put our protective stop

8. how to define the signal to get out

We will now look at answering those questions.

Solutions to the technical challenges of the strategy

1) What time frame to trade this strategy on

We will take trades off weekly charts, and expect trades to last from weeks to months.

2) How to define the overall market

We will use the FTSE All Share Index.

3) How to define "going up"

- Visual inspection, or

- ADX, or

- moving average combinations.

4) How to define relative strength versus the overall market

To enter a trade we will require the stock to have outperformed the overall market by at least 10% over the previous four weeks.

5) How to define relative strength versus the sector

To enter a trade we will require the stock to have outperformed the sector by at least 1% over the previous four weeks.

6) How to determine how much capital to risk

For all the examples we will assume we have total speculative funds of £20,000, and we will risk 1% on each trade (i.e. £200).

Note: This is a solution for traders who have mastered all the relevant techniques – less experienced traders should risk less than this (e.g. 0.25% or less).

---

7) How to determine where to put our protective stop

We will place our protective stop immediately below the low of the week of entry and the two previous weeks.

8) How to define the signal to get out

We will exit the trade if one of 4 events occur:

- the overall market direction changes from up to down (note, sideways is OK for this strategy provided the stock's outperformance of the overall market continues)

- the sector's direction changes from up to down (note, sideways is OK for this strategy provided the stock's outperformance of the overall market continues)

- the stock's end of week outperformance of the overall market over the previous four weeks is reduced to 1% or less for two weeks running

- our protective stop is hit

Example 1 – BG Group

The next four charts show the set up for this trade.

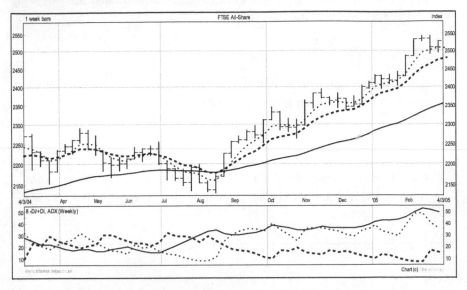

Visual inspection shows the All Share Index has been in a powerful up-trend. The moving averages are in up-trend mode. The ADX indicator is significantly above 25, with +DI above –DI.

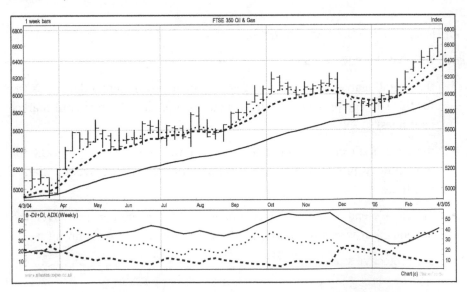

Visual inspection shows the Oil and Gas sector has been in a powerful up-trend. The moving averages are in up-trend mode. The ADX indicator is significantly above 25, with +DI above –DI.

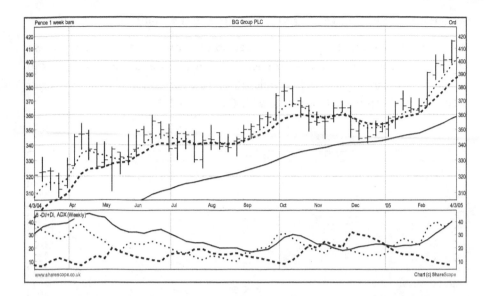

Visual inspection shows BG Group PLC has been in a powerful up-trend. The moving averages are in up-trend mode. The ADX indicator is significantly above 25, with +DI above –DI.

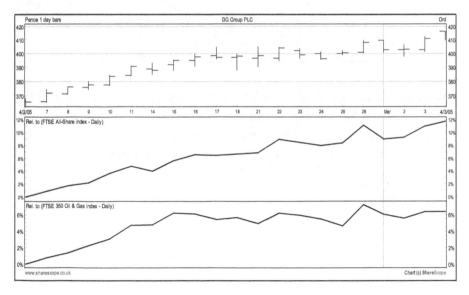

The daily chart shows that over the previous four weeks BG Group has outperformed the All Share Index by more than 10%. It has outperformed its sector, the Oil and Gas sector, by more than 1%.

We will go long first thing next week with a stop below the week of entry and the two previous weeks.

We enter the following week at 415.0p, with a stop at 390.25p.

Bets in BG Group are price in pounds per point, with a point being 1p, so we bet £8 per point. Since the distance between our entry and our stop is 24.75p this gives us a total risk on the trade of 24.75 x 8 = £198, in line with our predetermined cap on risk per trade of £200.

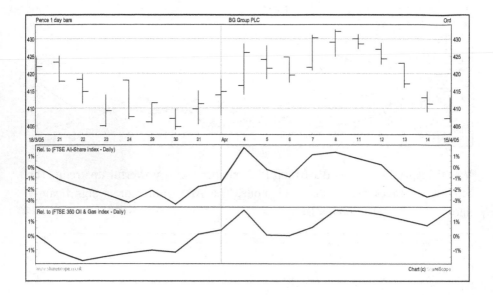

A warning sign has appeared: at the end of the week the outperformance of BG Group versus the All Share Index for the four previous weeks has dropped to 1% or worse (actually -2%). This is not yet a signal to exit, but if it is still at 1% or worse at the end of next week that will be a signal to exit.

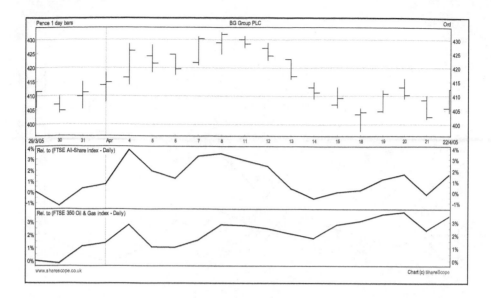

Outperformance just hanging on in there, at 1.5%, so no signal to exit yet.

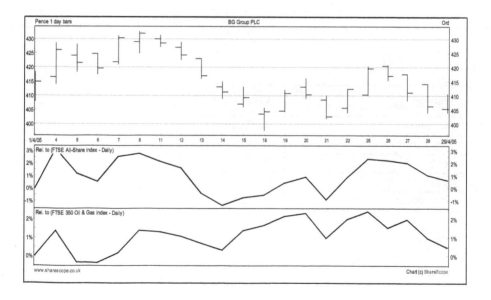

Outperformance has again dropped to 1% or worse, if it is still at 1% or worse at the end of next week that will be a signal to exit.

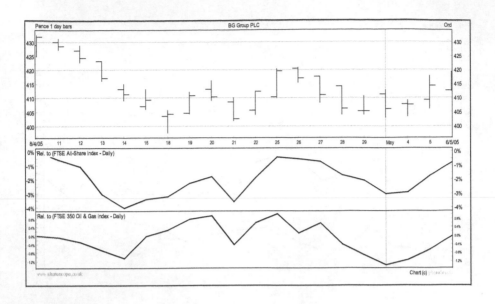

Outperformance at 1% or less for two weeks running, that is a signal to exit. We will exit when the markets open on Monday.

We exit at 419.25, for a miniscule profit.

Trade summary

Field	Value
Instrument	BG Group
Long / short	Long
Entry	415.0
£s per point	8
Protective stop	390.25
Exit	419.25
Risk (£s)	198
Risk as a % of trading capital	1.0
Profit (£s)	34
Profit-to-risk ratio	0.2
Percentage move	1.0
Length of trade (weeks)	9

Something quite straightforward has occurred: we entered a trade according to our system, and we exited the trade according to our system. We ended up effectively with a scratched trade (neither a profit nor a loss of any significance).

As it happens, after we exited the share renewed its up-trend and we could have made a good profit by hanging on longer.

It is important not to get agitated by this.

The art of trading is not to get the best result on every single trade, but to play a percentage game over a series of trades. This strategy trades outperformance. Outperformance on this trade had ceased, so the reason for our trade had disappeared. Time to move on and look for opportunities elsewhere.

Example 2 – Aquarius Platinum

Here are the four charts which provided the set up for this next trade. We are doing our research on a Thursday evening because we have the Easter weekend ahead of us, the markets will be shut on Friday and Monday.

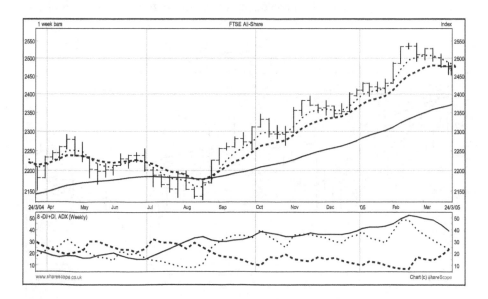

Visual inspection shows that the overall market has been in a strong up-trend, although there has been a pullback for the last five weeks or so. The pullback has caused the faster moving averages to turn down, but the overall configuration is still bullish. The pullback has also caused the ADX indicator to turn down, and –DI is getting close to crossing over +DI, however it has not done so yet.

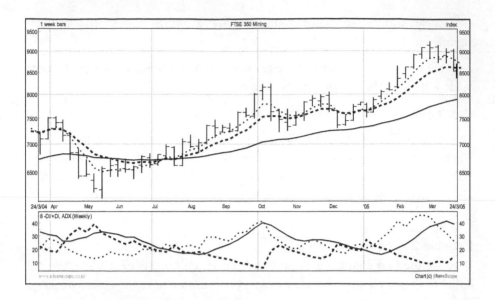

The chart of the Mining sector shows much the same tendencies as the All Share, a strong up-trend with a recent pullback, although the turn down of the ADX indicator is less pronounced.

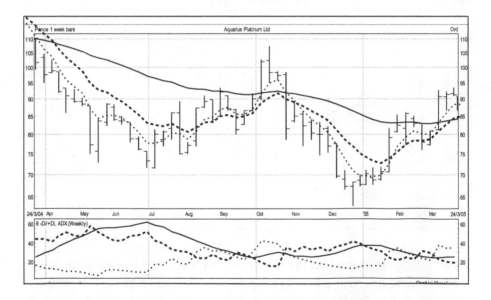

Visual inspection shows that Aquarius Platinum has been in an up-trend since the start of the year, although the price action taking the last twelve months as a whole looks somewhat rangebound. The moving average configuration has just become bullish per our definition for the first time in the last twelve months, with the 4 week average now above the 10 week and the 10 week above the 40 week. The ADX indicator (at 25) is fairly inconclusive at this point, although +DI is above –DI.

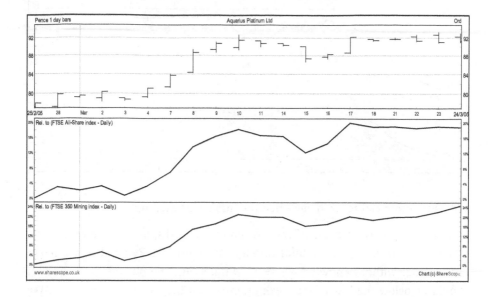

This chart shows why we are so interested in the stock.

It has outperformed the All Share by more than 18% over the last 4 weeks. It has also outperformed the Mining Index significantly. We will buy when the markets open on Tuesday, with a stop below the low of the entry week and the two previous weeks.

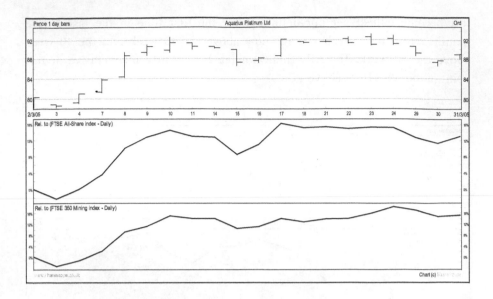

We had an interesting problem when the market opened on Tuesday.

Price opened below the low of the two previous weeks, and as we considered when to get in it kept on falling through the morning. Remember, we never enter a trade without knowing where we will get out, and our rules say the stop should be below the low of the week of entry and the two previous weeks. We decide not to enter the trade until we believe we have identified the low of the week.

As we neared the close of play on the 31st March price we believed we had done just that. On that day the low had been higher than the low of the previous day, the high was higher than the high of the previous day, and the market was heading in to a close that was higher than the previous day.

We bought fifteen minutes before the close at 89.0, with a stop below the low of the previous day at 86.5.

Bets in Aquarius Platinum are priced in pounds per point, which means pounds per penny. We bet £80 per point, risking a total of £200 on this trade (89 – 86.5 times 80).

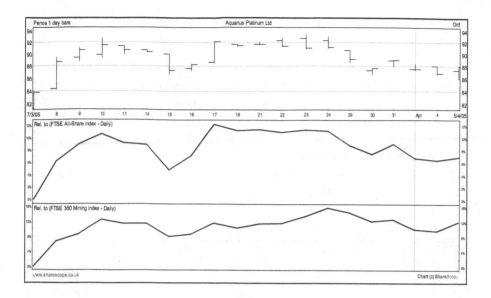

We were in this trade all of three days before our stop was hit.

In addition, our spread betting firm took us out of the trade at a worse price than our stop, due (they say in response to our query) to the market action at the time the stop was hit. We have access to intra day data which allows us to check this, and no valid reason for pursuing this issue further emerges.

Trade summary

Field	Value
Instrument	Aquarius Platinum Ltd
Long / short	Long
Entry	89.0
£s per point	80
Protective stop	86.5
Exit	86.0
Risk (£s)	200
Risk as a % of trading capital	1.0
Loss (£s)	240
Loss to risk ratio	1.2
Percentage move	3.4
Length of trade (weeks)	Less than 1

We congratulate ourselves for a job well done: the trade went against us and we got out promptly.

One of the keys to success in trading is to cut losses short and run winners. Unfortunately many traders prefer the opposite scenario, to bag their winners quickly and then hang on to their losers hoping they can turn them around.

Example 3 – Aquarius Platinum

Here are the four charts which provided the set up for this next trade, which is once again in Aquarius Platinum.

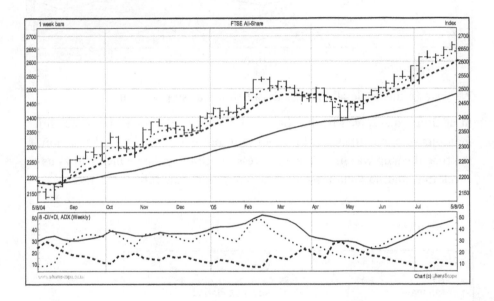

Visual inspection shows a strong up-trend and a new annual high. The moving averages are in up-trend mode, and the ADX indicator at 47 with +DI above –DI is also showing a strong up-trend.

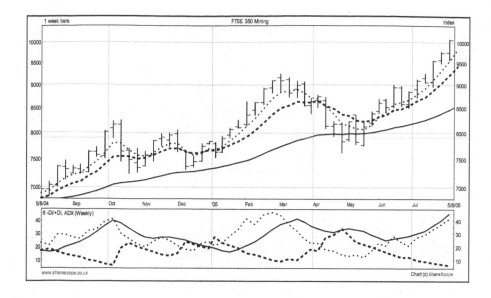

Visual inspection shows a strong up-trend and a new annual high. The moving averages are in up-trend mode, and the ADX indicator at 45 with +DI above –DI is also showing a strong up-trend.

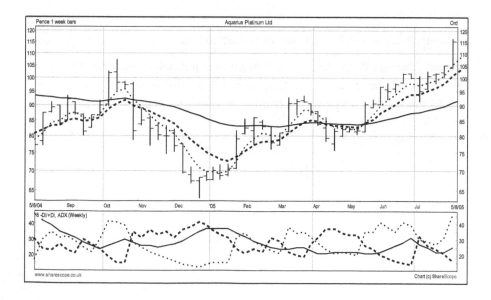

Visual inspection shows a strong up-trend and a new annual high. The configuration of the moving averages shows an up-trend. The ADX indicator, at 25, is showing at a borderline level between trending and not trending.

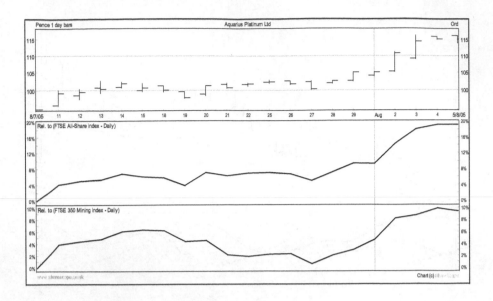

This chart shows why we are so interested in the stock.

It has outperformed the All Share by more than 19% over the previous 4 weeks. In addition it has outperformed the Mining sector. We will buy when the markets open on Monday, with a stop below the low of the entry week and the two previous weeks.

Our entry price is 114.75, and our stop is at 104.75.

Bets on Aquarius Platinum are price in pounds per point, which mean pounds per penny. We bet £20 per point, so our risk on this trade is £200 (114.75 – 104.75 times 20) – in line with our predetermined maximum risk per trade.

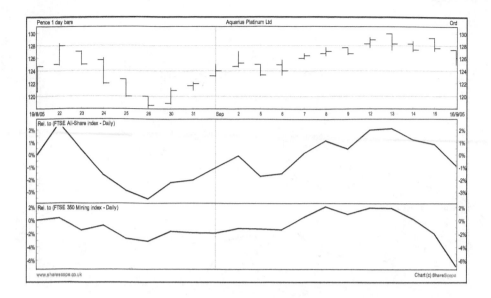

A warning sign: at the end of the week outperformance versus the All Share Index over the previous four weeks has dropped to 1% or less – if this is still the case at the close of next week we will have had a signal to exit the trade.

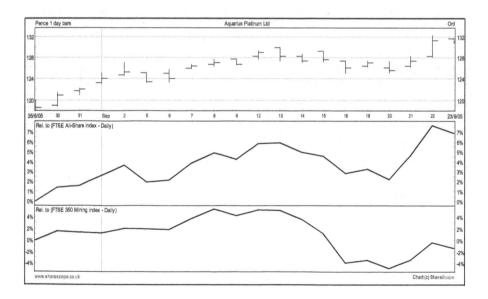

Back on track, no signal to exit.

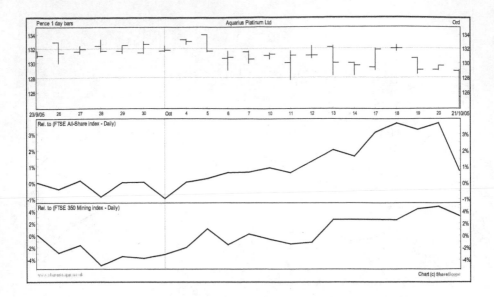

A warning sign: at the end of the week outperformance versus the All Share Index over the previous four weeks has dropped to 1% or less – if this is still the case at the close of next week we will have had a signal to exit the trade.

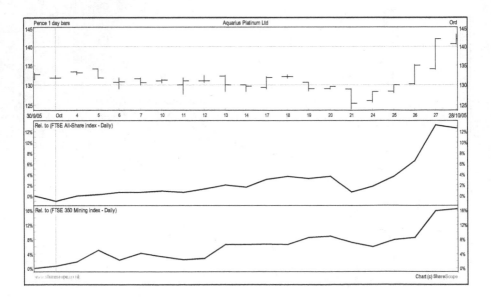

Back on track, no signal to exit.

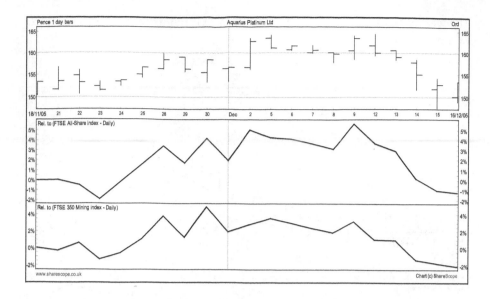

A warning sign: at the end of the week outperformance versus the All Share Index over the previous four weeks has dropped to 1% or less – if this is still the case at the close of next week we will have had a signal to exit the trade.

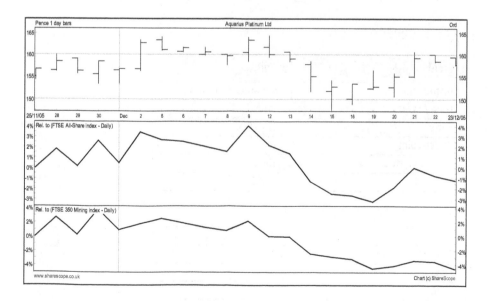

Two weeks running with outperformance at 1% or less – we have received a signal to exit. We will exit when the markets open on 28th December.

Our exit price is 157.5.

The weekly chart below shows our entry and exit points for this trade, marked by the arrows.

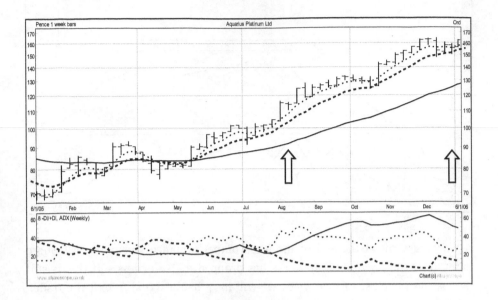

Trade summary

Field	Value
Instrument	Aquarius Platinum
Long / short	Long
Entry	114.75
£s per point	20
Protective stop	104.75
Exit	157.5
Risk (£s)	200
Risk as a % of trading capital	1.0
Profit (£s)	855
Profit-to-risk ratio	4.3
Percentage move	37.3
Length of trade (weeks)	21

A solid trade, lasting about five months, with a profit-to-risk ratio of 4.3. When the outperformance stopped we exited clinically, looking for other opportunities.

As it happens, after a further period of consolidation after we exited, this particular stock recommenced its outperformance and we were able to take another trade in the stock. Exiting a stock does not in any way preclude us from taking another trade in it at a later date.

Strategy 3 – Selling Rallies

Introduction to the strategy

This strategy is applicable to all asset classes. For stocks it is most effective when the overall market is clearly in bear mode, or when particular market sectors are clearly in bear mode. It also works well with other asset classes when the down-trend stands out. It gets in after the trend has already formed, and it tends to get out before it is over; it aims to get a piece of the action while controlling risk, rather than capturing the whole trend.

> *Note*: This strategy is the counterpart to the "buying dips" strategy we looked at earlier. Instead of buying on temporary weakness in an up-trend we are here aiming to sell on temporary strength in a down-trend.

Strategy methodology

The basic methodology of this strategy when applied to stocks is:

1. overall market is going down

2. the stock's sector is going down

3. the stock is going down

4. we wait for a short-term rally in the stock

5. we wait for the short-term rally to end

6. we calculate how much capital to risk on this trade

7. we determine where our protective stop will be

8. we calculate trade size based on 6 and 7

9. then we go short

10. we stay short until we get a signal to get out

There is a slight variation in this strategy for commodities, indices, bonds and currencies: the strategy starts at Step 3.

Advantages and disadvantages of the strategy

The main advantages of this strategy are:

- We are in accord with the overall direction of the market, the sector our stock is in and the stock itself. Market conditions are on our side, we are not fighting against them.

- By waiting for a short-term rally we get an improved entry price and can define a logical point for a stop, above the high of the rally.

- Our trade size is a function of how much we are prepared to risk and where our stop will be.

The main disadvantage of this strategy is that not all down-trends we want to take advantage of will provide us with the opportunity to enter after a short-term rally – we are going to miss some.

Technical challenges of the strategy

The main technical challenges in implementing this strategy are:

1. what time frame to trade this strategy on

2. how to define the overall market

3. how to define "going down"

4. how to define a short-term rally

5. how to define when the short-term rally has ended

6. how to determine how much capital to risk

7. how to determine where to put our protective stop

8. how to define the signal to get out

These questions are answered opposite.

Solutions to the technical challenges of the strategy

First we will look briefly at possible solutions to each of these technical challenges, and then the rest of this chapter will show examples of the strategy in action using a selection of the solutions.

1) What time frame to trade this strategy on

We will take trades off weekly charts, and expect trades to last from weeks to months.

2) How to define the overall market

We will use the FTSE All Share Index.

3) How to define "going down"

- Visual inspection, or
- ADX, or
- moving average combinations.

4) How to define a short-term rally

- 3 week RSI overbought, or
- a weekly high higher than at least the previous 2 weekly highs.

5) How to define when the short-term rally has ended

We will adopt the solution that it has ended when price falls beneath the previous week's low.

6) How to determine how much capital to risk

For all the examples we will assume we have total speculative funds of £20,000, and we will risk 1% on each trade (i.e. £200).

Note: This is a solution for traders who have mastered all the relevant techniques – less experienced traders should risk less than this (e.g. 0.25% or less).

---

7) How to determine where to put our protective stop

We will place our protective stop immediately above the high of the week of entry and the two previous weeks.

8) How to define the signal to get out

We have already determined that our protective stop is above the high of the last two weeks; if that is hit we will exit. Otherwise we will stay in the trade until either

- +DI climbs above –DI, suggesting the down-trend has ended, or
- at least one of the moving averages turns up, suggesting the down-trend is stalling.

Example 1 – BT Group PLC

Here are three charts showing the initial set up point for this trade.

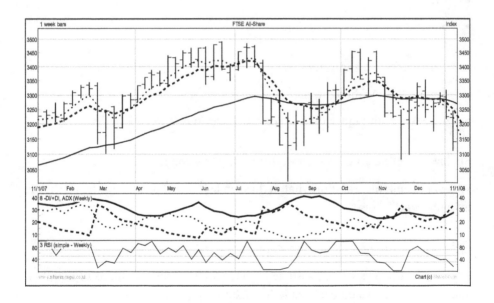

Moving averages in down-trend configuration. ADX above 25 with –DI above +DI.

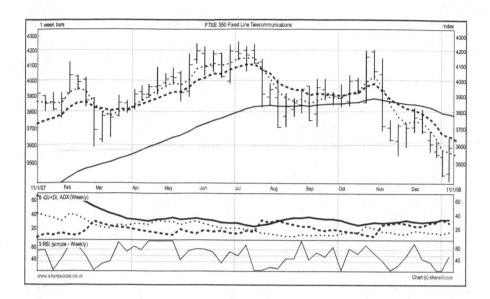

Moving averages in down-trend configuration. ADX above 25 with –DI above +DI.

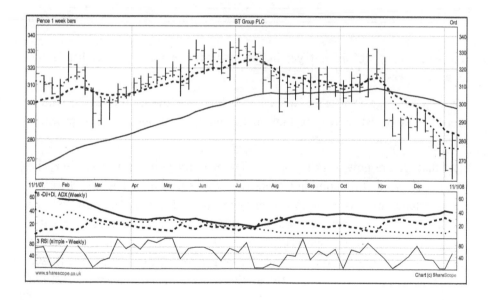

Moving averages in down-trend configuration. ADX above 25 with –DI above +DI.

Week's high is above previous two week's highs. We prepare to go short next week if price goes below this week's low, with a protective stop above the high of the entry week and the two previous weeks. The entry can be fully automated via a stop order to enter; and several providers also offer contingent orders which means the protective stop will also be placed automatically if our stop order to enter is filled.

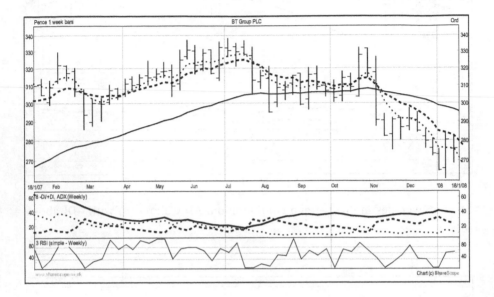

One week later, we are not yet in the trade (price failed to get below the previous weeks low).

We prepare to go short next week just below the low of this week, with a protective stop just above the high of the entry week and the two previous weeks.

Note that we are now working off a different entry point from last week, the distance between entry point and protective stop is now different, and therefore the calculation of how much to bet on this trade is different. Our entry will be at 268.25p, our protective stop will be at 284.5p. The difference between entry point and stop is 16.25p, and because we have predetermined that we want to risk approximately £200 on this trade we will therefore bet £12 per point (200 / 16.25) – actual risk £195 (12 x 16.25). We will sell the equivalent of £3219 of BT stock (12 x 268.25).

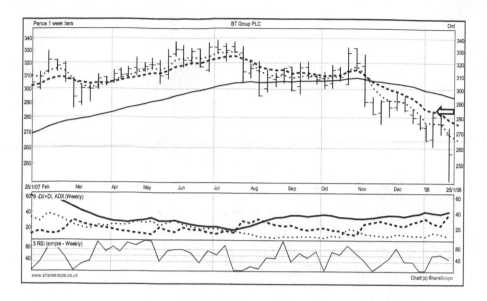

During the week (ending 25th January) our stop order to enter was triggered, we got into the trade at 268.25p, with a protective stop at 284.5p just above the high of the entry week and the two previous weeks (shown by the arrow).

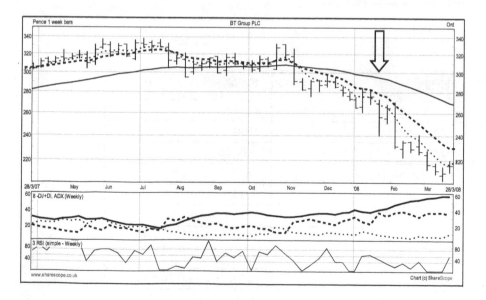

We have been in the trade for a couple of months, and it has gone well. The week we entered is shown by the arrow. The 4 week moving average is starting to flatten, but has not yet turned up decisively, so we have not yet had a signal to exit.

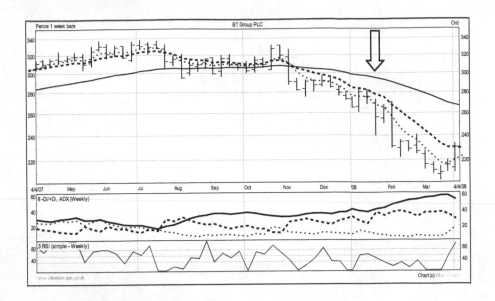

Now the 4 week moving average has turned up decisively, giving us our signal to exit. We will exit first thing on Monday morning. Note that the ADX indicator has turned down from a high level which can also be a warning sign that the trend is stalling.

Trade summary

Field	Value
Instrument	BT Group
Long / short	Short
Entry	268.25p
£s per point	12
Protective stop	284.5p
Exit	232.75p
Risk (£s)	195 (284.5-268.25 x12)
Risk as a % of trading capital	1.0
Profit (£s)	426 (268.25-232.75 x12)
Profit-to-risk ratio	2.2
Percentage move	13.2
Length of trade (weeks)	12

This strategy has got us a piece of the action in the down-trend. The ratio of profit-to-risk, while not spectacular, is OK. The down-trend had already started before we got on board, and we gave up some profits at the end, only getting out after the down-trend had stalled.

No problem!

This strategy is not designed to capture the whole of a move, just a good solid chunk of it. Although the down-trend had stalled at the point we exited it had not ended, and as it happens it was destined to continue with renewed vigour after it had finished stalling. Again, no problem! This strategy gets us out when the trend stalls, enabling us to reallocate capital elsewhere.

Example 2 – Dollar Yen, Trade 1

Here is a chart showing the set up for this trade.

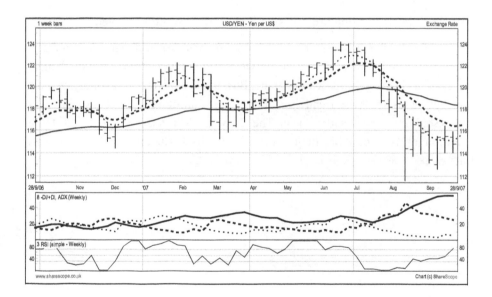

This currency pair shows how many Yen there are to 1 Dollar.

Visual inspection shows the big down-trend which followed the mid June highs around 124. ADX levels are well above 25 with –DI above +DI. But the down-trend has stalled a little, and the 3 week RSI has reached overbought levels above 75. We would like to go short if price hits 113.90, below the low of the week.

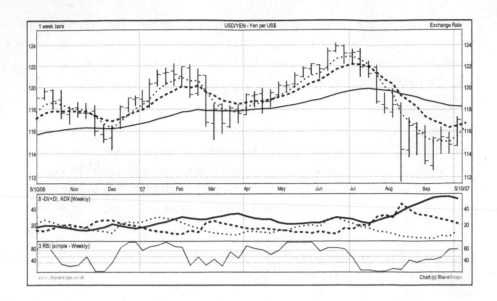

One week later, our stop order has not been filled, so no trade yet.

As the down-trend retraces, the ADX indicator has turned down, the two faster moving averages have turned up. If we were already short we would have received a clear signal to exit our trade. But our chosen technical analysis tools are telling us that the trend is stalling, not that it is over, so we are still interested in a new short trade. The 3 week RSI has become even more overbought. We would like to go short if price hits 114.60, below the low of this last week.

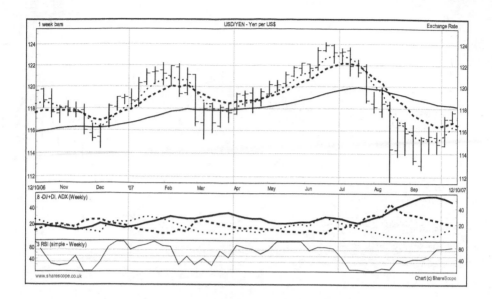

Another week, still not filled, still interested in a short trade.

We would like to go short if price hits 116.70, below the low of this last week. The 4 week moving average has not yet crossed above the 10 week moving average, so by our definition this is still a down-trend. If it does cross, signalling a sideways market, we will abandon our search here for a short trade.

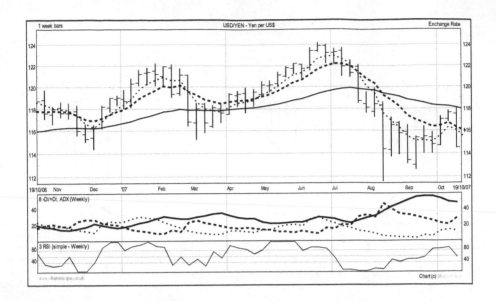

This week (ending 19 October) price did indeed hit 116.70, so we have gone short.

Our initial protective stop is at 118.10, above the high of the entry week and the two previous weeks. Dollar Yen bets are usually priced per 0.01 Yen, so we have bet £1 per 0.01 Yen, risking £140 (118.10 less 116.70, divided by 0.01).

Unfortunately our spread betting company only allows bets of whole numbers of pounds per 0.01 Yen, so our choice was between risking £140 (too little according to our system rules) and £280 (too much); we chose the more conservative option.

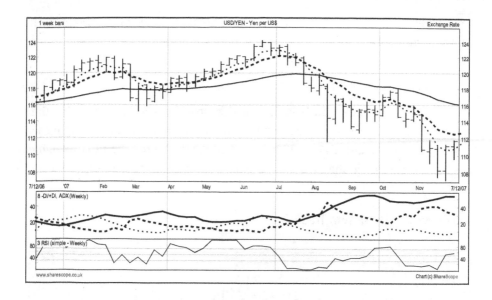

This week (ending 7th December) the 4 week moving average has turned up, giving us a signal to exit. We will exit as soon as the markets open next week.

Trade summary

Field	Value
Instrument	Dollar Yen
Long / short	Short
Entry	116.70
£s per point	1
Protective stop	118.10
Exit	111.60
Risk (£s)	140
Risk as a % of trading capital	0.7
Profit (£s)	510
Profit-to-risk ratio	3.6
Percentage move	4.4
Length of trade (weeks)	8

This trade provided us with an opportunity to participate in the Dollar Yen down-trend, getting us in after a temporary lull in the down-trend, then allowing us to get out as a small retracement started.

The profit-to-risk ratio of 3.6 is very acceptable.

We wanted to reallocate our capital once the trend started stalling. But this down-trend is not necessarily over for good, and there is nothing stopping us getting back on board it again if it gets going once more. The next example shows how we can do that, waiting patiently on the sidelines for a new set up.

Example 3 - Dollar Yen, Trade 2

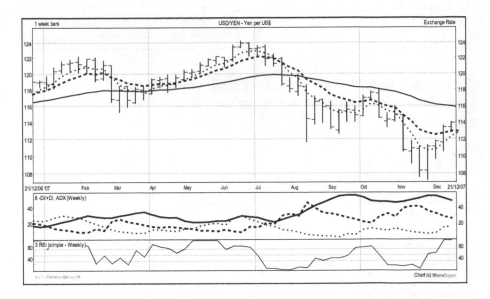

This is the chart a couple of weeks on from where we exited our previous Dollar Yen short trade.

The 10 week moving average has turned up as well as the 4 week moving average, and we have preserved our capital (and our previous profits) by being out of the market during this retracement. But moving average configuration has not yet moved from down-trend to sideways (the 4 week moving average has not yet crossed up over over 10 week). The ADX indicator is still signalling a down-trend. And the 3 week RSI is overbought. We are interested in a new short trade if price can take out the low of the previous week.

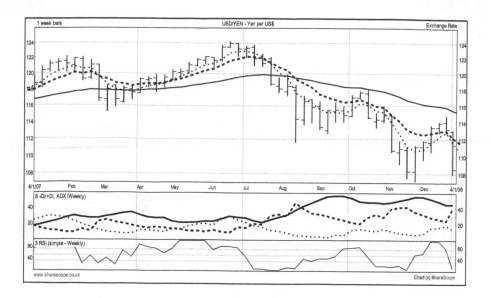

Another two weeks on, and this week (ending 4th January) we entered a new short trade in Dollar Yen, as price dropped below the low of the previous week. Our entry price was 112.60. Our protective stop, above the high of the entry week and the two previous weeks is at 114.80.

Unfortunately this gives us a risk marginally above our predetermined £200, at £220, once again there is the issue of having to bet a whole number of pounds per 0.01 Yen. We decided that this risk was just within our tolerance levels. Given that the trade has moved very quickly in our favour at the end of the week we move our stop to 114.60, thereby now limiting our risk to £200 as desired.

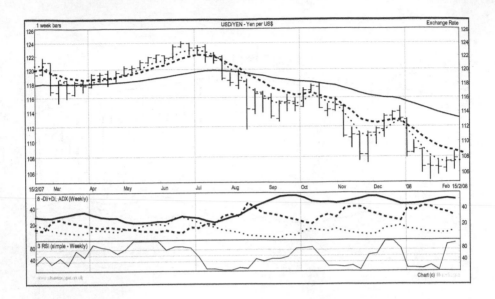

The shorter moving averages have flattened, but have not yet moved up, so no signal to exit yet.

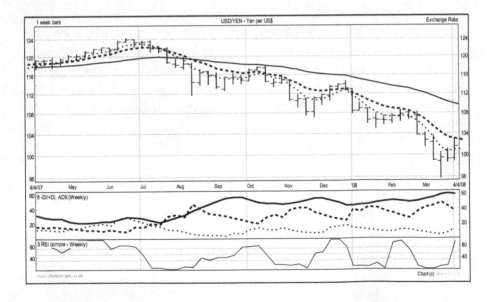

The 4 week moving average looks like it is beginning to turn up, but it is not a decisive turn up; perhaps some traders would now exit, but for better or worse we decide to stick with the trade for another week.

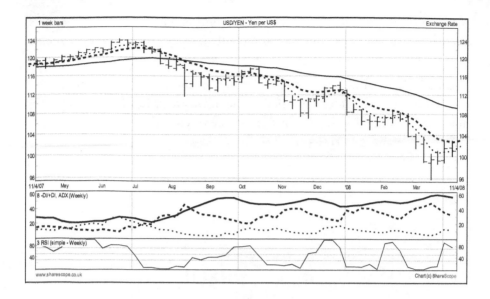

OK, enough is enough.

The 4 week moving average has definitely turned up, and the 10 week moving average is starting to. Time to exit this trade. We will exit as soon as the markets open next week.

Trade summary

Field	Value
Instrument	Dollar Yen
Long / short	Short
Entry	112.60
£s per point	1
Protective stop	114.80
Exit	101.10
Risk (£s)	220
Risk as a % of trading capital	1.1
Profit (£s)	1150
Profit-to-risk ratio	5.2
Percentage move	10.2
Length of trade (weeks)	15

A 5.2 profit-to-risk ratio is a very useful contribution to the output of this strategy. A few trades like this should more than compensate for the inevitable losing trades.

This trade followed on from another Dollar Yen short trade, and between the two trades we have successfully ridden the down-trend for the best part of 6 months, with just a few weeks out during a retracement.

Strategy 4 – Selling Relative Weakness

Introduction to the strategy

This strategy is for stocks. It is most effective when the market and the stock's sector are both in clear down-trends. It shorts stocks which are underperforming market and sector, and stays short as long as the relative weakness continues.

Note: This is the counterpart to the buying relative strength strategy we looked at earlier. Instead of buying relative strength in a bull market we are here aiming to sell relative weakness in a bear market.

Strategy methodology

The basic methodology of this strategy is:

1. overall market is going down

2. the stock's sector is going down

3. the stock is going down

4. the stock is weak relative to the overall market and the sector

5. we calculate how much capital to risk on this trade

6. we determine where our protective stop will be

7. we calculate trade size based on 5 and 6

8. then we go short

9. we stay short until we get a signal to get out.

Advantages and disadvantages of the strategy

The main advantages of this strategy are:

- We are in accord with the overall direction of the market, the sector our stock is in and our stock. Market conditions are on our side, we are not fighting against them.

- Our trade size is a function of how much we are prepared to risk and where our stop will be.

- The strategy can capture significant portions of an established down-trend.

The main disadvantages of this strategy are that while relative weakness continues it tends to ride out periods of consolidation and of retracement, rather than exiting; and it will also miss out on continuations of a down-trend when relative weakness ceases.

Technical challenges of the strategy

The main technical challenges in implementing this strategy are:

1. what time frame to trade this strategy on

2. how to define the overall market

3. how to define "going down"

4. how to define relative weakness versus the overall market

5. how to define relative weakness versus the sector

6. how to determine how much capital to risk

7. how to determine where to put our protective stop?

8. how to define the signal to get out

We will now look at answering these questions.

Solutions to the technical challenges of the strategy

1) What time frame to trade this strategy on

We will take trades off weekly charts, and expect trades to last from weeks to months.

2) How to define the overall market

We will use the FTSE All Share Index.

3) How to define "going down"

- Visual inspection, or
- ADX, or
- moving average combinations.

4) How to define relative weakness versus the overall market

To enter a trade we will require the stock to have underperformed the overall market by at least 10% over the previous four weeks.

5) How to define relative weakness versus the sector

To enter a trade we will require the stock to have underperformed the sector by at least 1% over the previous four weeks

6) How to determine how much capital to risk

For all the examples we will assume we have total speculative funds of £20,000, and we will risk 1% on each trade (i.e. £200).

Note: This is a solution for traders who have mastered all the relevant techniques – less experienced traders should risk less than this (e.g. 0.25% or less).

---

7) How to determine where to put our protective stop

We will place our protective stop immediately above the high of the last two weeks.

8) How to define the signal to get out

We will exit the trade if one of 4 events occur:

- the overall market direction changes from down to up (note, sideways is OK for this strategy provided the stock's underperformance of the overall market continues)

- the sector's direction changes from down to up (note, sideways is OK for this strategy provided the stock's underperformance of the overall market continues)

- the stock's underperformance of the overall market is reduced to less than 1% for two weeks running

- our protective stop is hit.

Example 1 – Alliance and Leicester

Here are the four charts showing the set up for this trade.

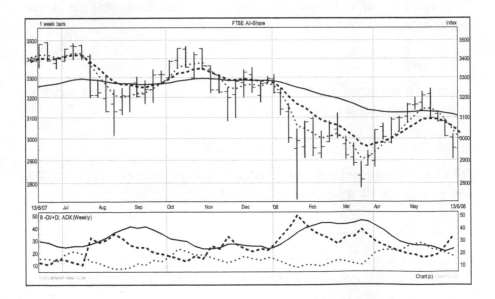

Visual inspection shows an overall decline across the last 12 months. The high made in late May is lower than highs made earlier in the year, and price has been falling for the last three weeks since then. The moving averages are now in bearish configuration, with the 4 week average below the 10 week, and the 10 week below the 40 week. The ADX indicator is indecisive (23) although –DI is above +DI.

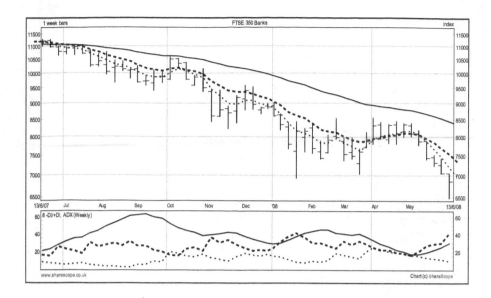

Visual inspection, the moving average configuration and the ADX indicator configuration all point to a powerful down-trend in the Banks index.

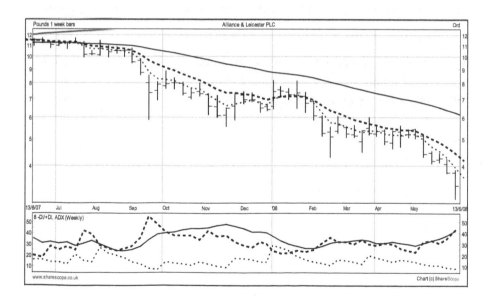

Visual inspection, the moving average configuration and the ADX indicator configuration all point to a powerful down-trend in the stock Alliance and Leicester PLC.

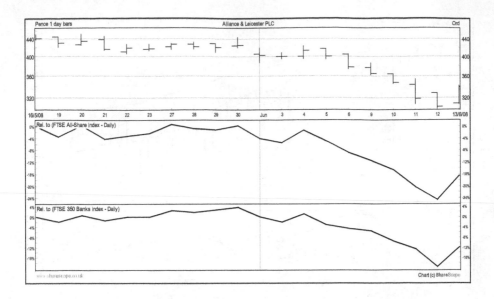

This chart shows why we are interested in this stock. It has underperformed the All Share index by more than 16% over the last 4 weeks, and it is also significantly underperforming the Banks index. We will enter on Monday at the open, with a stop above the high of the entry week and two previous weeks.

Our entry is at 345.5p, and our stop is at 424.0p.

Bets in this stock are priced in pounds per point, which is the same as pounds per penny. We bet £2 per point, risking £157 (424 - 345.5 times 2). Betting £3 per point would give us a risk of £235.50, which is too far above our predetermined maximum risk per trade.

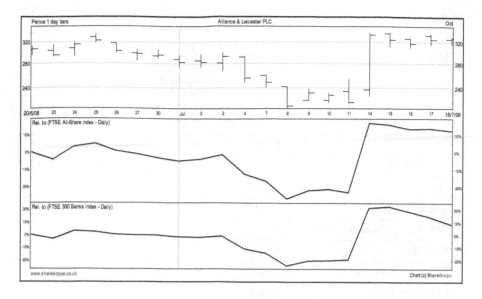

At the end of the week underperformance versus the All Share Index over the last four weeks is at 1% or worse – in fact the share has outperformed the Index by over 10%. If this situation persists to the end of next week we will exit. We are protected in the meantime by our stop which is very close to the high of the previous week.

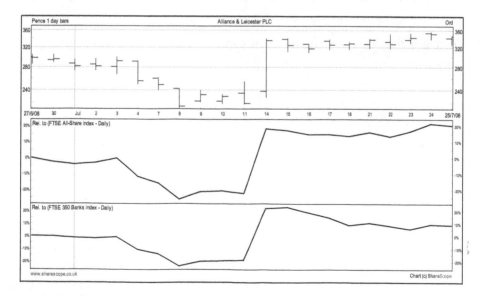

We have received our signal to exit, the stock has underperformed the All Share Index by less than 1% for two weeks running – in fact it has significantly outperformed it. We will exit as soon as the markets open next week.

Trade summary

Field	Value
Instrument	Alliance & Leicester PLC
Long / short	Short
Entry	345.5
£s per point	2
Protective stop	424.0
Exit	343.75
Risk (£s)	157
Risk as a % of trading capital	0.8
Profit (£s)	3.5
Profit-to-risk ratio	0.0
Percentage move	0.5
Length of trade (weeks)	6

This has turned out to be a scratched trade – neither a profit nor a loss of any significance. At one point in the trade price got down to 213.25, at which point we had a paper profit of £132, just over 80% of the total risked on the trade. This strategy has us holding out for more than that.

There is always the risk in trading that paper profits will disappear as we try to run our winners.

Example 2 – Persimmon

The next four charts show the set up for this trade.

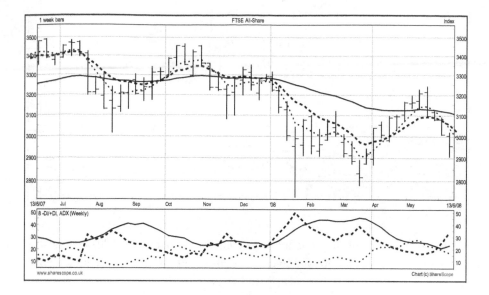

The set-up for this trade occurred at the same time as the previous example – so we start with the same position in the overall market, repeated here for convenience.

Visual inspection shows an overall decline across the last 12 months. The high made in late May is lower than highs made earlier in the year, and price has been falling for the last three weeks since then. The moving averages are now in bearish configuration, with the 4 week average below the 10 week, and the 10 week below the 40 week. The ADX indicator is indecisive (23) although –DI is above +DI.

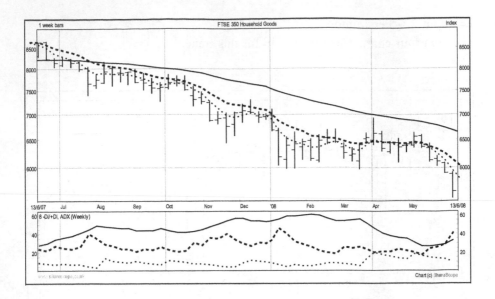

Visual inspection: the moving average configuration and the ADX indicator configuration all point to a powerful down-trend in the Household Goods Index.

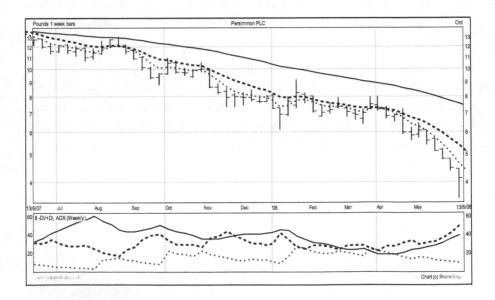

Visual inspection: the moving average configuration and the ADX indicator configuration all point to a powerful down-trend in the stock Persimmon PLC.

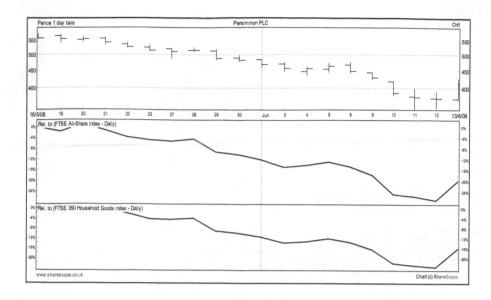

This chart shows why we are interested in this stock. It has underperformed the All Share index by around 20% over the last 4 weeks, and it is also significantly underperforming the Household Goods Index. We will enter on Monday at the open, with a stop above the high of the entry week and two previous weeks.

Our entry price is 415.0p. Our stop is 482.5p.

Bets in Persimmon are priced in pounds per point, which is the same as pounds per penny. We bet £3 per point, so our risk is £202.50 (482.5 – 415 times 3), in line with our predetermined risk per trade.

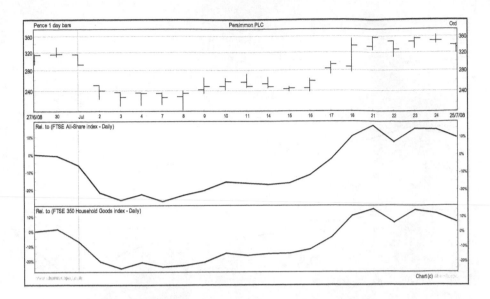

At the end of the week underperformance versus the All Share Index over the previous four weeks is worse than 1% – in fact the share has significantly outperformed the index. If this situation remains the same at the end of next week we will have had a signal to exit.

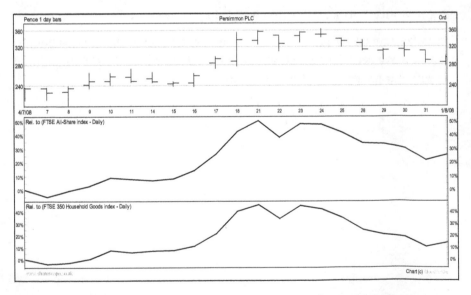

Two weeks running with underperformance versus the All Share Index over the previous four weeks worse than 1% (significantly worse), so that is is our signal to exit at the start of the next week.

Our exit price is 285.25p.

Trade summary

Field	Value
Instrument	Persimmon PLC
Long / short	Short
Entry	415.0
£s per point	3
Protective stop	482.5
Exit	285.25
Risk (£s)	202.5
Risk as a % of trading capital	1.0
Profit (£s)	389.25
Profit-to-risk ratio	1.9
Percentage move	31.3
Length of trade (weeks)	7

An OK trade, but nothing special, with a reward-to-risk ratio of 1.9.

At one point in this trade price dropped to 208.5p, at which point we had paper profits of £619.5. A powerful rally in the stock meant that some of those profits were eroded. Short covering can produce powerful moves, as all the traders who have placed short bets head for the exit at the same time.

There is a trade off in designing strategies, whether to go for quick and small profits relative to the risk taken or whether to shoot for larger profits with the associated risk of losing some of them in the process.

Example 3 – Galiform

The next four charts show the set up for this trade.

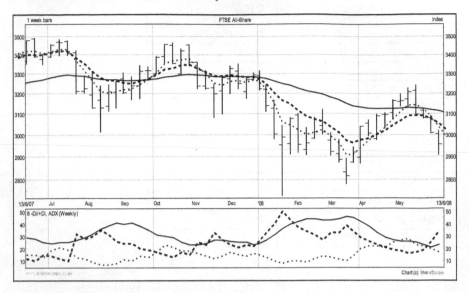

The set up for this trade occurred at the same time as the previous example – so we start with the same position in the overall market, repeated here for convenience.

Visual inspection shows an overall decline across the last 12 months. The high made in late May is lower than highs made earlier in the year, and price has been falling for the last three weeks since then. The moving averages are now in bearish configuration, with the 4 week average below the 10 week, and the 10 week below the 40 week. The ADX indicator is indecisive (23) although –DI is above +DI.

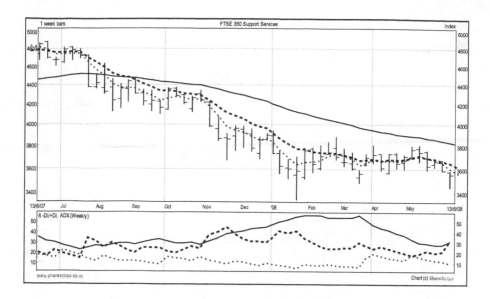

Visual inspection: the moving average configuration points to a powerful down-trend in the Support Services Index and the ADX indicator is in down-trend mode.

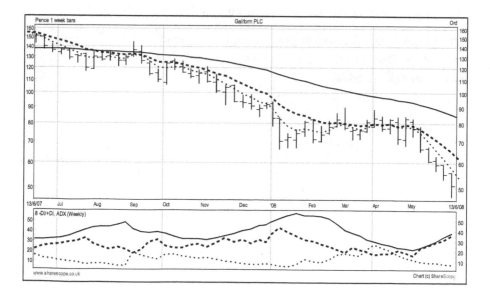

Visual inspection: the moving average configuration and the ADX indicator configuration all point to a powerful down-trend in the stock Galiform PLC.

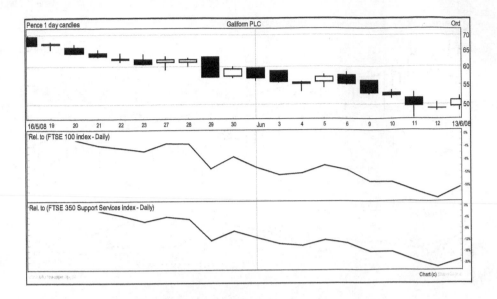

This chart shows why we are interested in this stock. It has underperformed the All Share index by over 16% over the last 4 weeks, and it is also significantly underperforming the Support Services Index. We will enter on Monday at the open, with a stop above the high of the entry week and two previous weeks.

Our entry price is 52.25p. Our stop is at 59.75p.

Bets on this stock are priced in pounds per point (penny). We bet £26 per point. Our risk is £195 (59.75 – 52.25 times 26), in line with our predetermined maximum risk per trade.

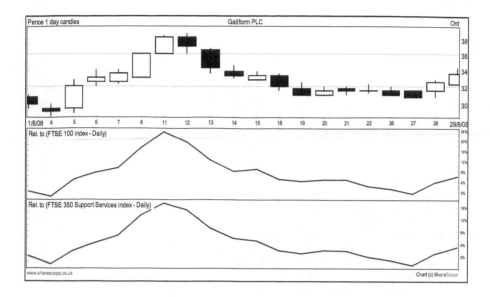

At the end of the week underperformance of the All Share Index has fallen below 1% (in fact the stock has outperformed the Index significantly). If this happens again at the end of next week that will be a signal to exit.

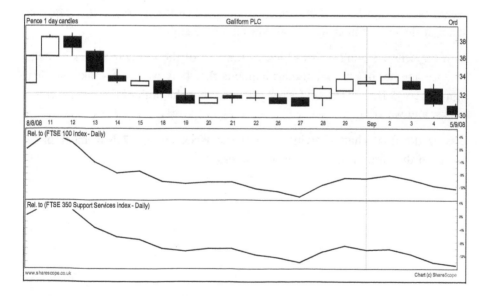

Underperformance resumed, no signal to exit.

We now move ahead almost two months.

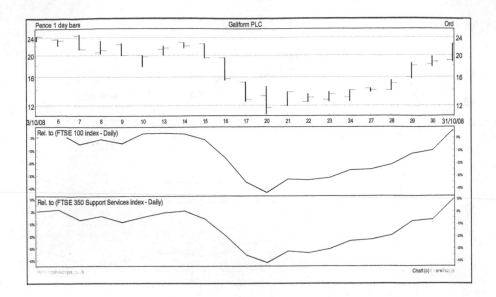

At the end of the week underperformance of the All Share Index has fallen below 1% (in fact the stock has outperformed the Index slightly). If this happens again at the end of next week that will be a signal to exit.

At the end of the week underperformance of the Sector has also fallen below 1% (in fact the stock has significantly outperformed the sector). If this happens again at the end of next week that will also be a signal to exit.

As it happens we don't wait as long as the end of the following week to exit, because another of our exit signals happens first (and we always take the first signal to exit). During the next week price exceeds the high of the two previous weeks, and we are out.

Here is the final chart showing that in the week ending 7 November price exceeded the high of the two previous weeks.

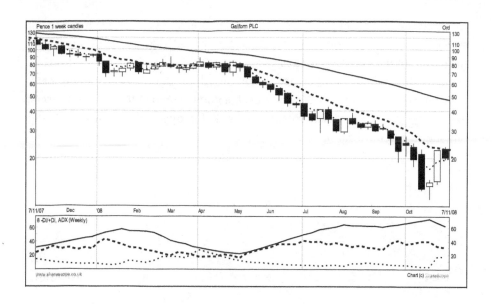

Trade summary

Field	Value
Instrument	Galiform PLC
Long / short	Short
Entry	52.25
£s per point	26
Protective stop	59.75
Exit	22.75
Risk (£s)	195
Risk as a % of trading capital	1.0
Profit (£s)	767.00
Profit-to-risk ratio	3.9
Percentage move	56.5
Length of trade (weeks)	20

The risk/reward ratio on this trade was an acceptable 3.9. to 1.

An interesting practical point occurs with this trade. Supposing we had not got stopped out, and the price had fallen to, say, 7p. At that point the maximum further profit possible would have been £182 (7 x 26; stocks cannot fall below zero). With maximum further profit now less than the amount we originally risked it would have almost certainly been a good idea to exit even if no formal exit signal had been given; to go and look for opportunities with a better ongoing risk/reward ratio.

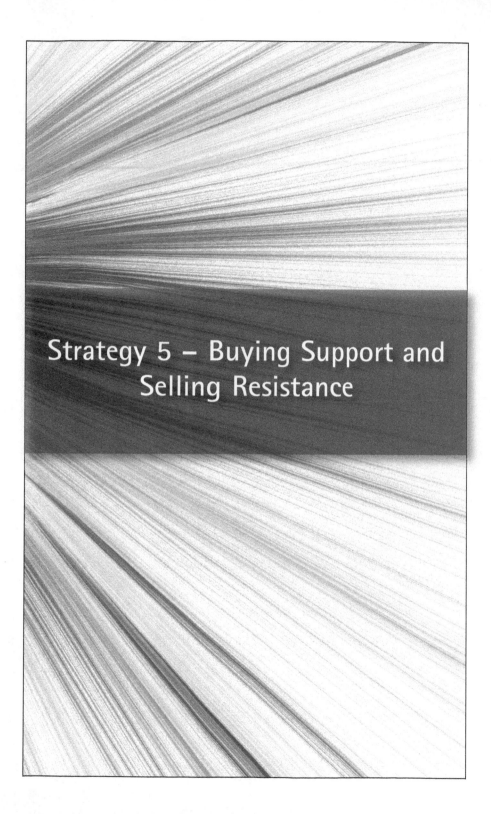

Strategy 5 – Buying Support and Selling Resistance

Introduction to the strategy

Markets trend up or down less than half the time. This strategy trades when there is no clear trend up or down, buying support and selling resistance. It works best when support and resistance levels are clear, the more traders see these levels the more likely it is they will act on them. These are fairly short trades; the intention is just to take the ride from support to resistance, or from resistance to support – so the distance between support and resistance needs to be big enough to make the trade worthwhile.

Strategy methodology

The basic methodology of this strategy when applied to stocks is:

1. overall market is going sideways

2. the stock's sector is going sideways

3. the stock is going sideways

4. there are clear support and resistance levels

5. we wait for price to get near support or resistance

6. we calculate how much capital to risk on this trade

7. we determine where our protective stop will be

8. we calculate trade size based on 6 and 7

9. we go long at support or go short at resistance

10. we move our protective stop as the trade goes in our favour

---

Note: There is a slight variation in this strategy for commodities, indices, bonds and currencies: the strategy starts at Step 3.

Advantages and disadvantages of the strategy

The main advantages of this strategy are:

- We can make money when the overall market is going sideways.

- Our trade size is a function of how much we are prepared to risk and where our stop will be.

- This strategy aims for small but quick profits.

The main disadvantage of this strategy is that when support or resistance is broken price often moves swiftly against us, it is essential with this strategy to be able to exit immediately if our initial stop is hit.

Technical challenges of the strategy

The main technical challenges in implementing this strategy are:

1. what time frame to trade this strategy

2. how to define the overall market

3. how to define "going sideways"

4. how to define support and resistance

5. how to determine how much capital to risk

6. how to determine where to put our protective stop

7. how to define the signal to get out

We will now look at answering these questions.

Solutions to the technical challenges of the strategy

1) What time frame to trade this strategy on

We will take trades off weekly charts, and expect trades to last from one week to a few weeks.

2) How to define the overall market

We will use the FTSE All Share Index.

3) How to define "going sideways"

- ˙Visual inspection, or
- ADX, or
- moving average combinations.

4) How to define support and resistance

- Visual inspection, or
- weekly pivots.

5) How to determine how much capital to risk

For all the examples we will assume we have total speculative funds of £20,000, and we will risk 1% on each trade (i.e. £200).

Note: This is a solution for traders who have mastered all the relevant techniques – less experienced traders should risk less than this (e.g. 0.25% or less).

---

6) How to determine where to put our protective stop

We will place our protective stop below the support level when buying support or above the resistance level when selling resistance.

7) How to define the signal to get out

We will adopt a trailing stop solution: once price has reached the halfway point between support and resistance we will trail our protective stop:

- if we have **bought support** we will trail a stop *below* the low of the previous two weeks

- if we have **sold resistance** we will trail a stop *above* the high of the two previous weeks.

Once price has reached the other side of the range we will tighten the stop further:

- if we have **bought support** we will trail a stop *below* the low of the last week

- if we have **sold resistance** we will trail a stop *above* the high of the last week.

Example 1 – Sterling Dollar

The next chart shows the set up for this trade.

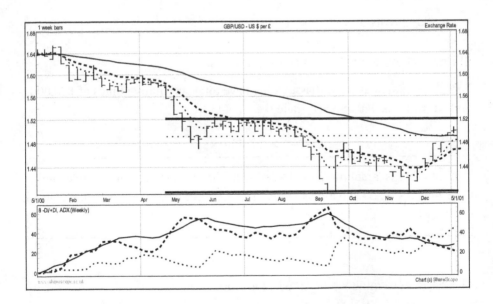

Visual inspection shows that the Sterling Dollar currency pair has been rangebound since early June, trading between a high around 1.52 and a low around 1.40. These levels are marked with thick lines on the chart. The resistance at 1.52 is strong in that price has had three goes at getting above it and failed each time. At the support level price has got down to 1.40 twice, and has then recovered strongly on both occasions. There is a gap between the third from last and the penultimate price bar, no trades took place at prices between the high of one bar and the low of the next, which is usually a bullish development; however the price action since then has stalled, and in this last week in particular price has ended at roughly the same level as it started after attempting to rise during the week.

Visual inspection also shows that most of the trading between June and mid-August was contained within a very narrow band, ranging from the 1.52 resistance at the top end to around 1.4920 at the bottom end. The 1.4920 level is marked by the horizontal dotted line on the chart. Price is now stalling in that old narrow band.

The moving average configuration is in sideways mode. The recent climb from the bottom of the trading range has pushed the ADX indicator level up marginally above 25 (27) with +DI above –DI.

The reasons to take a short trade now are:

1. price is nearing resistance levels

2. the distance from the latest price to support is several times the distance from the latest price to resistance, making the reward-to-risk ratio attractive

3. visual inspection suggests the move up from support is now stalling

4. visual inspection suggests that the old narrow band near resistance will act as resistance

We will enter when the markets open next week.

Our entry price is 1.4970.

Our stop is at 1.5170, at the top end of the old narrow band near resistance. If price can get all the way up to there we probably don't want to stay short.

Sterling dollar bets are priced in pounds per 0.0001 dollar. We risk £1 per 0.0001 dollar. Our risk on this trade is £200, in line with our predetermined maximum exposure per trade (1.5170 – 1.4970 divided by 0.0001).

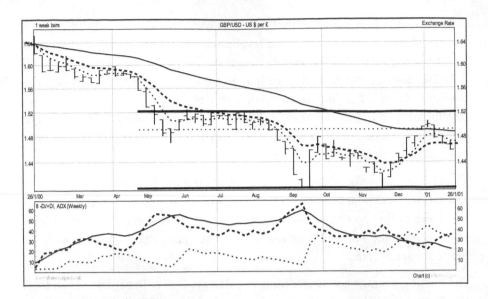

Three weeks in to the trade and price has now hit the halfway point between the upper and the lower limits of the trading range, which is 1.46.

Following the rules of this strategy, we now move our protective stop to just above the high of the last two weeks. We move the stop from 1.5170 to 1.4810, thereby locking in a profit of £160 (1.4970 – 1.4810).

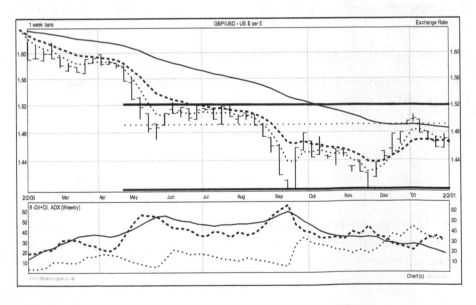

Our trailing stop is moved down to just above the high of the last two weeks, down to 1.4780, now locking in a profit of £190.

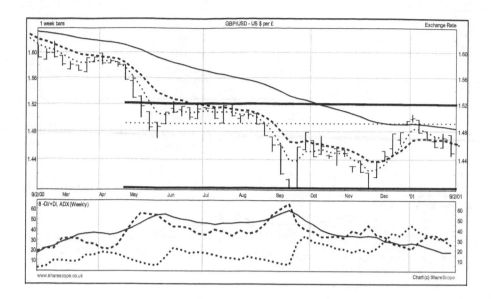

No change to our trailing stop this week, since the high of the last two weeks has not changed.

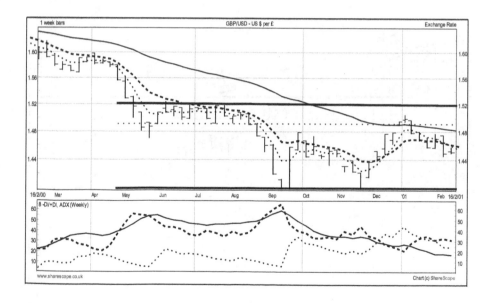

Our trailing stop is moved down to just above the high of the last two weeks, down to 1.4760, locking in a profit of £210.

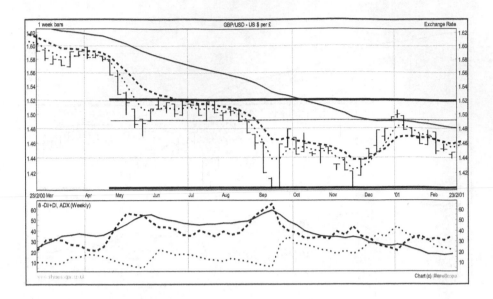

Our trailing stop is moved down to just above the high of the last two weeks, down to 1.4590, locking in a profit of £380.

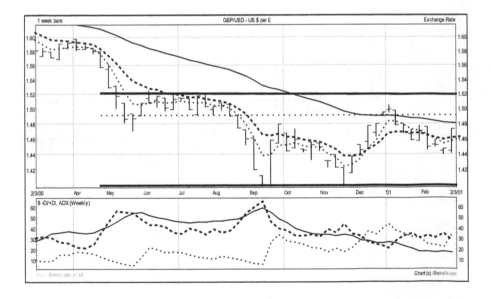

Our stop has been hit this week, as price climbed above the high of the two previous weeks.

Trade summary

Field	Value
Instrument	Sterling Dollar
Long / short	Short
Entry	1.4970
£s per point	1
Protective stop	1.5170
Exit	1.4590
Risk (£s)	200
Risk as a % of trading capital	1.0
Profit (£s)	380
Profit-to-risk ratio	1.9
Percentage move	2.5
Length of trade (weeks)	8

A reasonable result for this type of trade, a reward-to-risk ratio of 1.9.

At the end of the trade there was still some way to go to the bottom end of the trading range. We were holding out for more, but once we were in the bottom half of the range we made sure we locked in a good proportion of our existing paper profits by using a trailing stop.

Example 2 – Euro Dollar

The next chart shows the set up for this trade.

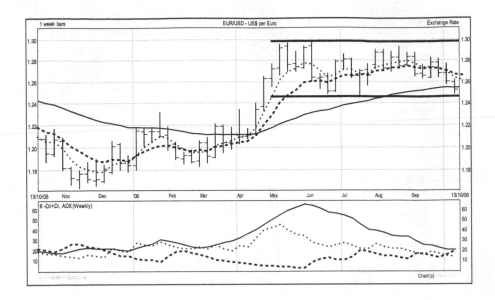

Visual inspection shows that the currency pair Euro Dollar has been rangebound since early May, with the upper end of the range just under 1.30, and the lower end of the range between 1.24 and 1.25. Both the moving average configuration and the ADX configuration point to a sideways range. In addition, for those that look to geometric patterns, the whole of the trading range could be construed as a flag formation, following the run up from 1.17, a formation which is more often than not a continuation pattern.

There are several reasons to go long:

1. price is near the bottom of the trading range;

2. from the current price level, the distance to the top of the range is significantly greater than the distance to the bottom of the range, producing a favourable reward-to-risk ratio for a long trade;

3. the flag formation, if we see it as valid, places some emphasis on the long side.

We will go long at the open next week, with a stop below the lowest support level of the trading range.

Our entry price is 1.2510. Our stop is at 1.2450.

Bets on Euro Dollar are priced in pounds per 0.0001 Dollar. We bet £3 per Dollar. Our risk is £180 (1.2510 – 1.2450 divided by 0.0001, times 3). This is in line with our predetermined maximum risk per trade.

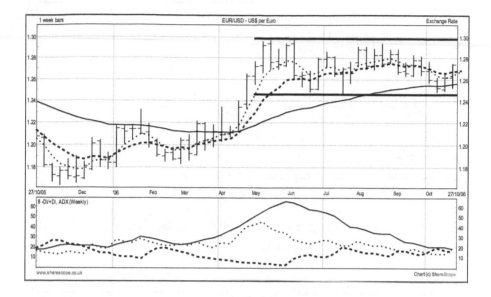

Price has now reached the half way point between the upper and lower limits of the trading range (at 1.2720), so in line with the rules of the strategy we now move our stop to just under the low of the last two weeks. Our stop is moved to 1.2480, limiting our risk on the trade now to £90 (1.2510 – 1.2480 divided by 0.0001, times 3).

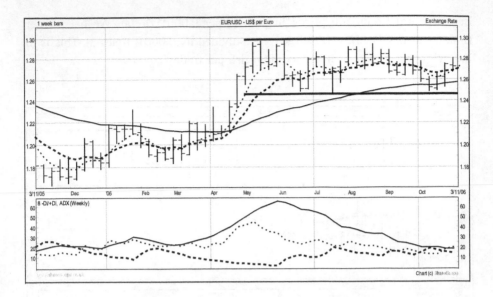

We move our stop again to just below the low of the last two weeks, to 1.2510, now guaranteeing a break even trade at worst.

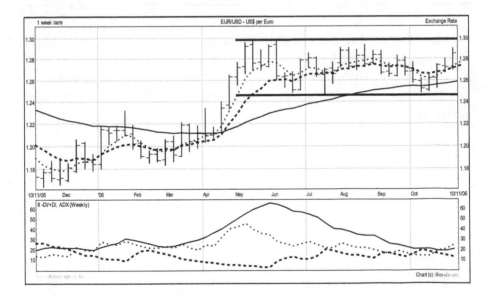

We move our stop again to just below the low of the last two weeks, to 1.2670, locking in a profit of £480.

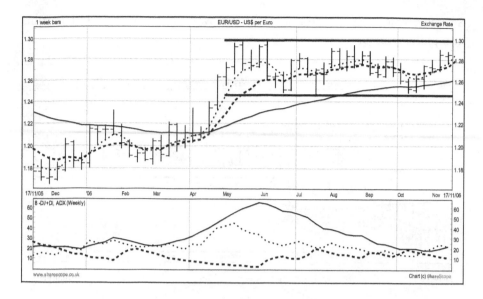

We move our stop again to just below the low of the last two weeks, to 1.2680, locking in a profit of £510.

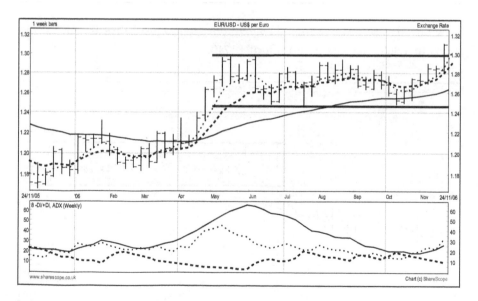

Something new has occurred – we were taking a trade from one side of a trading range to the other, now price has broken out of the trading range, in our favour. Some traders would have already exited at the upper level of the trading range, for them that was all they ever planned to do, the trade is over. Our strategy at this stage locks in more profits by tightening the stop to just below the low of the week, and then gives us a rare chance to hold out for a huge win.

So we now move our stop to just below the low of the week, to 1.2790, locking in a profit of £840.

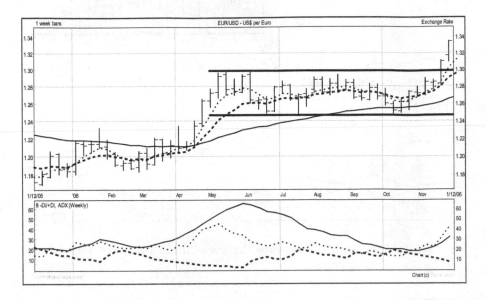

Now price has surged upwards. We move our stop to just below the low of the week, to 1.3080, locking in a profit of £1710.

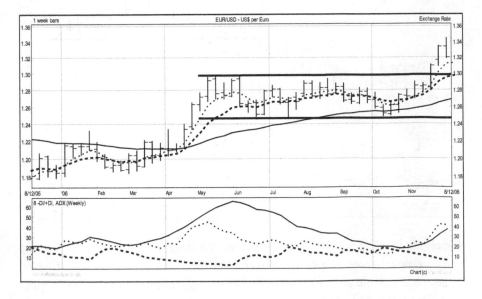

Now move our stop again to just below the low of the week, to 1.3180, locking in a profit of £2010.

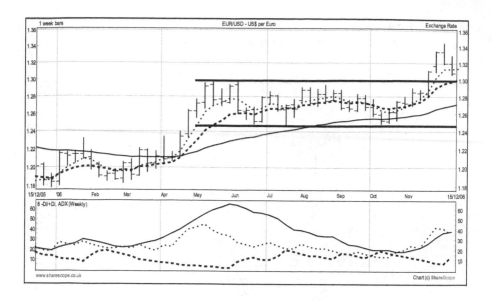

During the week our stop was hit, and we exited at 1.3180.

Trade summary

Field	Value
Instrument	Euro Dollar
Long / short	Long
Entry	1.2510
£s per point	3
Protective stop	1.2450
Exit	1.3180
Risk (£s)	180
Risk as a % of trading capital	0.9
Profit (£s)	2010
Profit-to-risk ratio	11.2
Percentage move	5.4
Length of trade (weeks)	9

Our strategy allowed us to convert a trade from one side of a trading range to the other into a break out trade. As a result the ratio of profit-to-risk is very high for this type of trade, at 11.2.

Example 3 – Dollar Yen

The next chart shows the set up for this trade.

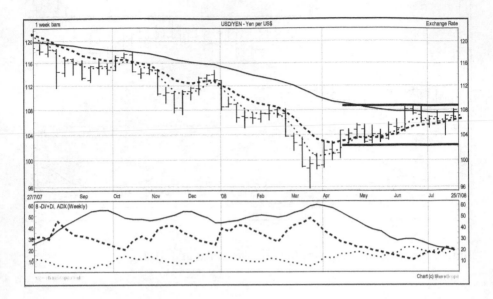

Visual inspection shows the Dollar Yen currency pair rangebound, with the upper limit of the range between 108 and 109, and the lower limit between 102 and 103. (Shown by the two thick black lines on the chart). In addition the 108 to 109 level had also provided resistance back in February.

The moving average configuration and the ADX configuration both show a sideways market.

The reasons to enter a short trade are:

1. price is at the upper end of the range;

2. from the latest price, the distance to the upper limit of the range compared to the distance to the lower limit of the range offers a good reward-to-risk ratio for a short trade;

3. the 108-109 level has provided resistance earlier in the year.

We will enter when the markets open next week.

The entry price is 108.40, and we place our stop above the top of the resistance level, at 108.62.

Bets in Dollar Yen are priced in pounds per 0.01 Yen. We bet £9 per 0.01 Yen. Our risk is £198, in line with our predetermined maximum risk per trade (108.62 – 108.40 divided by 0.01, times 9).

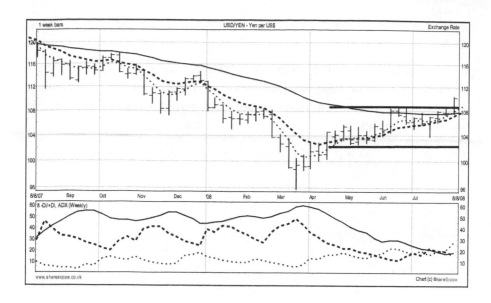

During the week price rose to the level of our stop, so we have exited the trade.

Trade summary

Field	Value
Instrument	Dollar Yen
Long / short	Short
Entry	108.40
£s per point	9
Protective stop	108.62
Exit	108.62
Risk (£s)	198
Risk as a % of trading capital	1.0
Loss (£s)	198
Loss to risk ratio	1.0
Percentage move	0.2
Length of trade (weeks)	2

This had looked a good trade when we entered it. There was strong resistance above our entry level and we had been able to go short close to that resistance, which had set up an excellent reward-to-risk ratio if price had moved back to the bottom of the trading range.

When price penetrated that resistance level the market gave us the clearest possible signal that on this trade we were wrong. Penetration of a long standing resistance level like this can lead to a powerful move in what would be for us the wrong direction.

This strategy demands prompt exits when the trade goes against us like this.

Strategy 6 – Long / Short Portfolio

Introduction to the strategy

This strategy is for stocks and is based on the observation that markets trend up or down less than half the time. The strategy generates trades when there is no clear trend up or down in the overall market. The aim is to hold a mixture of long and short positions with no net exposure to the overall market. This strategy works best when some sectors are in a clear up-trend and others are in a clear down-trend.

Strategy methodology

The basic methodology of this strategy is:

1. overall market is going sideways

2. at least one sector is going up and at least one sector is going down

3. some stocks in the sector(s) going up are outperforming the overall market and some stocks in the sector(s) going down are underperforming the overall market

4. we determine how many stocks to have in our long / short portfolio

5. we calculate how much capital to risk per stock in the long / short portfolio

6. we determine where our protective stop will be for each stock

7. we calculate trade size based on 5 and 6

8. we create our portfolio

9. we have rules for replacing stocks in the portfolio

10. we have rules for discontinuing the portfolio

Advantages and disadvantages of the strategy

The main advantages of this strategy are:

*   We can make money when the overall market is going sideways.

*   Our trade size is a function of how much we are prepared to risk and where our stops will be.

*   This strategy is able to ride sector trends while the overall market is not moving.

The main disadvantage of this strategy is that it is a little more complex than the others presented in this book, with more variables and more decisions required by the investor.

Technical challenges of the strategy

The main technical challenges in implementing this strategy are:

1. what time frame to trade this strategy

2. how to define the overall market

3. how to define "going sideways", "going up" and "going down"

4. how to define "outperforming" and "underperforming" the overall market

5. how to determine how many stocks to have in the portfolio

6. how to determine how much capital to risk per stock

7. how to determine where to put our protective stops

8. how to define the signal to exit and replace individual stocks in the portfolio

9. how to define the signal to discontinue the portfolio

We will now look at answering those questions.

Solutions to the technical challenges of the strategy

1) What time frame to trade this strategy on

We will take trades off weekly charts, and expect trades to last from weeks to months.

2) How to define the overall market

We will use the FTSE All Share Index.

3) How to define "going sideways", "going up" and "going down"

- Visual inspection, or
- ADX, or
- moving average combinations.

4) How to define outperforming and underperforming the overall market

To go long of a stock we will require the stock to have outperformed the overall market by at least 5% over the previous four weeks; once in a trade we will require outperformance of at least 1% over the last four weeks; to go short of a stock we will require the stock to have underperformed by at least 5% over the previous four weeks; once in a trade we will require underperformance of at least 1% over the last four weeks.

5) How to determine how many stocks to have in the portfolio

We will have just 2 stocks in the portfolio, 1 long and 1 short.

6) How to determine how much capital to risk per stock

For all the examples we will assume we have total speculative funds of £20,000, and we will risk 1% on each trade (i.e. £200).

Note: This is a solution for traders who have mastered all the relevant techniques – less experienced traders should risk less than this (e.g. 0.25% or less).

Total exposure across both stocks will therefore be 2%, i.e. £400.

7) How to determine where to put our protective stops

We will place our protective stops immediately below the low of the entry week and the two previous weeks for longs, immediately above the high of the entry week and the two previous weeks for shorts.

8) How to define the signal to exit and replace individual stocks in the portfolio

We will adopt the following conditions for replacing stocks in the portfolio

1. the stock's direction changes from up to sideways or down (for longs) or from down to sideways or up (for shorts), or

2. the stock's overperformance/underperformance of the overall market is reduced to less than 1% for two weeks running, or

3. our protective stop is hit.

9) How to define the signal to discontinue the portfolio

We will discontinue the portfolio immediately if the overall market moves into an up-trend or into a down-trend.

Example 1 – Diageo & Shire

The following seven charts show the set up for this trade.

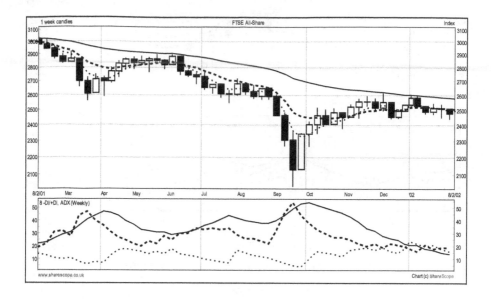

Visual inspection shows that the FTSE All Share index has been going sideways for about 4 months. The ADX indicator is a low level (14), with +DI and –DI criss crossing each other. The moving averages are in sideways mode, although close to down-trend mode.

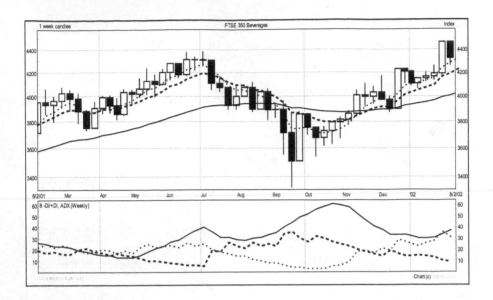

Visual inspection: the ADX configuration and the moving average configuration all point to an up-trend in the Beverages sector.

The ADX configuration and the moving average configuration show the Pharmaceutical sector in a down-trend. Visual inspection reveals a choppy down-trend, with some sideways action in recent weeks.

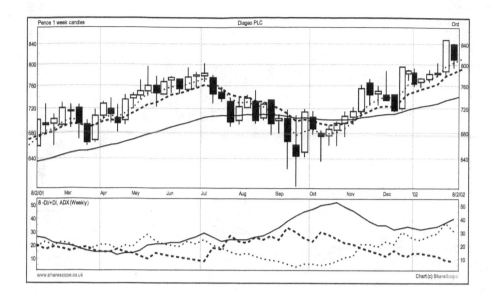

The stock Diageo PLC (ticker code DGE, and a constituent of the Beverages sector) is in a clear powerful up-trend...

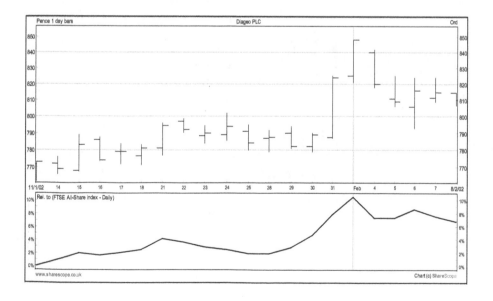

...and Diageo has outperformed the market by over 5% over the last 4 weeks.

The stock Shire Ltd (ticker code SHP, and a constituent of the Pharmaceuticals sector) is in a clear down-trend...

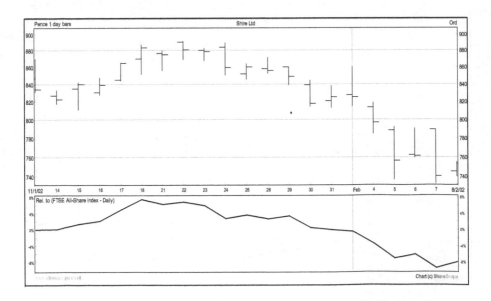

...and Shire has underperformed the market by over 5% over the last 4 weeks.

Next week, at the open, we will go long Diageo, short Shire, equalising our risk across the two stocks. Our protective stops are predetermined per the rules outlined earlier.

Until spread betting firms offer fractions of pounds per point as standard it will be rare to be able to match the risk exactly on the long and short legs of this strategy.

- We enter long Diageo at 803p with a stop at 778p, nine pounds a point, risking £225.

- We enter short Shire at 756p with a stop at 872p, two pounds a point, risking £232.

The total risk is a little above our budget, there was a trade off with this set up of risking a little over budget or a lot under budget (if we risked £1 per point on SHP).

The next four charts show the position three months later.

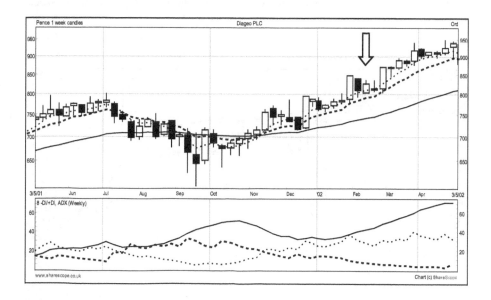

The arrow marks the week we entered long, and the up-trend is still in force.

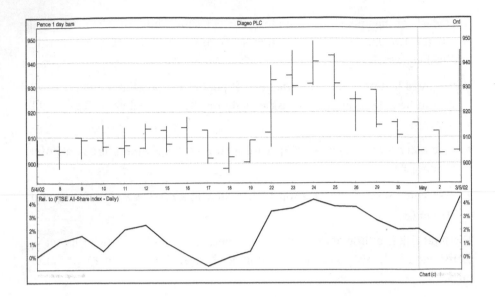

Here is the chart showing Diageo's performance versus the overall market, which is above the 1% outperformance threshold we have set to keep the stock in our portfolio.

The arrow marks the week we entered short. The down-trend is still in force, however it looks like the +DI line may soon cross over the –DI line.

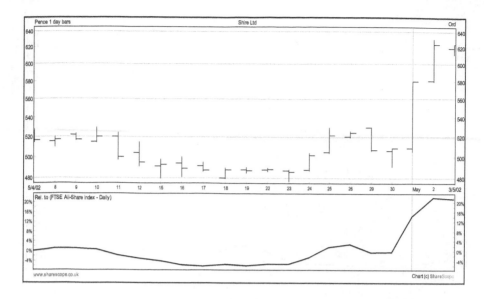

Here is the chart showing Shire's performance versus the overall market, which is the opposite of what we want – significant outperformance over the last four weeks rather than at least 1% underperformance. If this is still the situation next week this will be our signal to close down this trade.

The +DI line has indeed crossed over the –DI line, so under one of our definitions this is no longer a down-trend. Since the moving average configuration and visual inspection still indicate a down-trend we do not yet have a clear signal to exit from this chart.

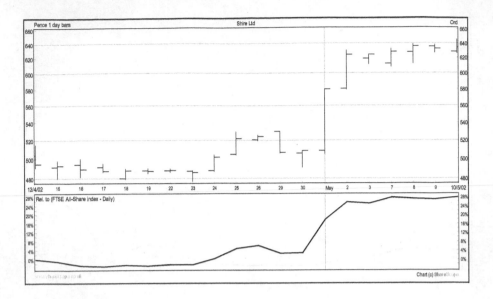

For the second week in a row Shire has missed our underperformance threshold by a long way, giving us our signal to exit. We will exit at the open next week.

My personal preference is to regard this as the end of one trade. The overall market at this point is still in sideways mode, and we still have an open long in Diageo, with no reason to exit. So we will carry forward our long in Diageo into the next trade, and we will therefore need to find a suitable new short trade to complete the portfolio. Although in practice we will just keep the long trade open, to complete our analysis of this example we will "clock it out" of this trade, and clock it back in to the next one at next week's opening price.

The short in Shire is closed at 628p.

Trade summary

Field	Value
Instrument	DGE and SHP
Long / short	Long DGE, short SHP
Entry	DGE 803, SHP 756
£s per point	DGE 9, SHP 2
Protective stop	DGE 778, SHP 872
Exit	DGE (carried forward) 870, SHP 628
Risk (£s)	DGE 225, SHP 232, total 457
Risk as a % of trading capital	DGE 1.1, SHP 1.2
Profit (£s)	DGE 603, SHP 256, total 859
Profit-to-risk ratio	DGE 2.7, SHP 1.1, total 1.9
Percentage move	DGE 8.3, SHP 16.9
Length of trade (weeks)	13

In a sense, this is an interim report, since we are carrying over the long trade. The strategy has enabled us to participate in two sector trends, one long one short, while the overall market has been going sideways. The 1.9 to 1 reward-to-risk ratio may not seem earth shattering, but this strategy is really a holding play while we wait for the overall market to start a new up-trend or down-trend.

Example 2 – Diageo & Aviva

We already have the long portion of this trade, carried over from the previous example. We are long Diageo at 870, 9 pounds a point, based on an original risk of £225. We will continue to monitor the stock for exit signals in line with the strategy rules. We need an additional short trade to balance the portfolio.

Here are the four charts which lead us to our choice for that short trade.

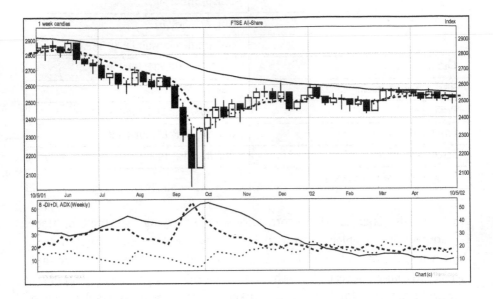

The overall market is still very much in sideways mode.

The Life Insurance sector is clearly in a down-trend, using all three of our criteria.

Aviva PLC (ticker code AV., and a constituent of the Life Insurance sector) is clearly in a down-trend, using all three of our criteria

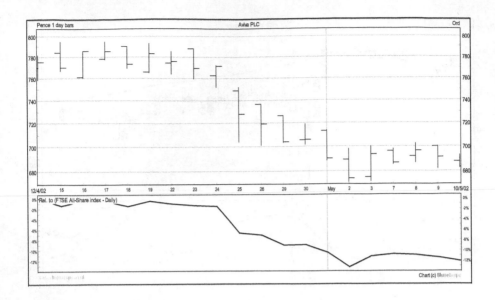

Aviva has underperformed the overall market over the last four weeks by significantly more than our 5% criterion.

We will enter short at the open next week. Our stop will be above the high of the entry week and the two previous weeks.

Our entry price is 696p and our stop is at 727p. We bet £7 a point, risking £217 on the trade, close to the original risk on our long trade.

One thing not yet mentioned, in the week that we received our signal to exit our existing short and replace it with Aviva, our long for the first time underperformed the overall market. So if at the end of the next week Diageo has not reached the threshold of 1% outperformance of the overall market, that will be our signal to exit.

This is the situation one week on.

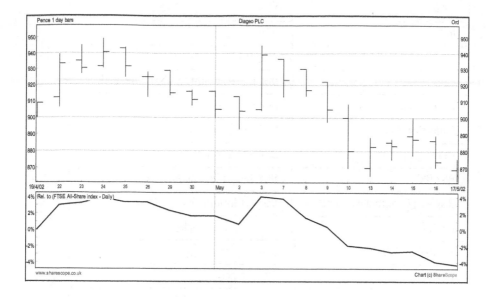

For the second week running **Diageo** has underperformed the overall market. We will exit at the open next week. The overall market is still going sideways, and our short trade is still valid, so our task is to find a replacement long trade to complete the portfolio, which we look at in example 3

As before we will tally up the score at this point. The stock Aviva is continuing in the portfolio but we clock it out in this example and clock it back in again in example 3.

The price achieved on the sale of **Diageo**, and the carry forward price of Aviva are reflected in the table below.

Trade summary

Field	Value
Instrument	DGE
Long / short	Long DGE,
Entry	DGE 870 (brought forward) , AV. 696
£s per point	DGE 9, AV. 7
Protective stop	DGE still @ 778, AV. 727
Exit	DGE 873, AV. 688 (carried forward)
Risk (£s)	DGE 225 (original), AV. 217
Risk as a % of trading capital	DGE 1.1 (original), AV. 1.1
Profit (£s)	DGE 3 (this example), AV. 8, total 11
Profit-to-risk ratio	Close to zero
Percentage move	Close to zero
Length of trade (weeks)	1

There has only been one week from introducing a new short trade into the portfolio to getting the signal to replace the long trade. There is no obvious connection between the two events, and sometimes there will be many weeks between the two.

Example 3 – Aviva & Imperial Tobacco

Example 3 has a start date just one week after example 2. The overall market and both the sector chart and the individual chart for our short trade have not changed in any material way. Our task is to select a new long trade for the portfolio.

Here are the three charts which lead to that decision.

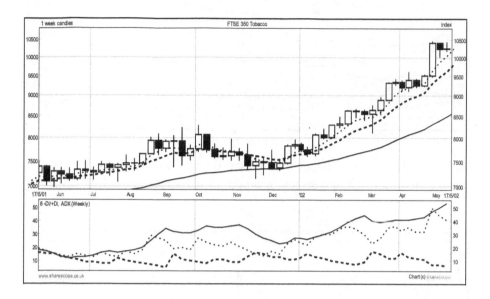

All our criteria show that the Tobacco sector is in a powerful up-trend.

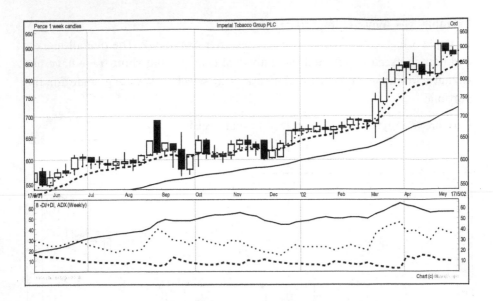

All our criteria show Imperial Tobacco Group PLC (ticker code IMT, a constituent of the Tobacco sector) in a powerful up-trend.

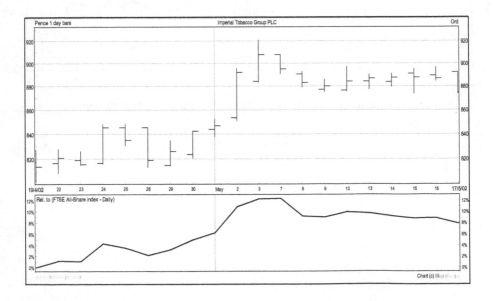

Imperial Tobacco has outperformed the overall market by significantly over 5% over the last 4 weeks. We will enter long at the open next week.

Our entry price is 884p, our stop (below the low of the entry week and the two previous weeks) is at 872p. We bet eighteen pounds a point, risking £216.

Both our long and our short trade progress well for six weeks, but then we receive an important signal concerning the overall market.

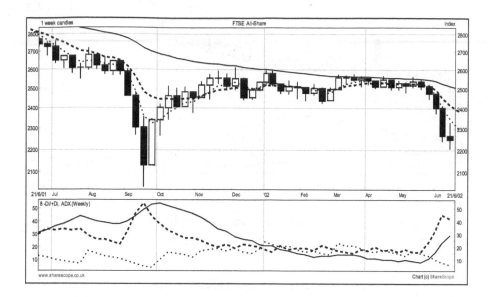

The overall market has clearly changed from sideways to down. The ADX indicator has risen to 29, with –DI moving strongly above +DI. Both visual inspection and the moving average configuration indicate a down-trend. This is our signal to stop using this strategy. At this point our long and our short still conformed to the required criteria of this strategy, but it is time to move on. This strategy is only for use in sideways markets, we no longer have a sideways market, we have other strategies for when the market is in a down-trend.

Out of interest, the next two charts show the position of our two stocks at the time that we pulled the plug on both of them, exiting at the open the following week. The exit prices achieved are reflected in the trade summary below.

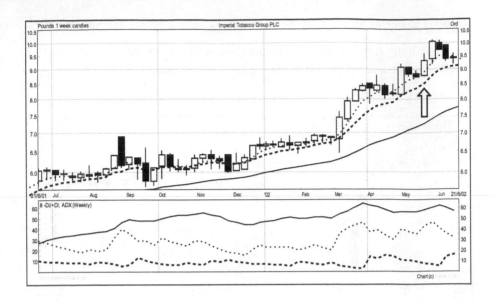

The arrow marks the start point for example 3. Still a healthy up-trend now, but time to exit, according to the rules of the strategy.

The arrow marks the start point for example 3. Still a powerful down-trend now, but time to exit, per the rules of the strategy.

Trade summary

Field	Value
Instrument	IMT , AV.
Long / short	Long IMT, short AV.
Entry	IMT 884, AV. 688 (brought forward)
£s per point	IMT 18, AV. 7
Protective stop	IMT 872, AV. 727 (original)
Exit	IMT 950, AV. 510
Risk (£s)	IMT 216, AV. 217 (original), total 433
Risk as a % of trading capital	IMT 1.1, AV. 1.1 (original)
Profit (£s)	IMT 1188, AV. 1246, total 2434
Profit-to-risk ratio	IMT 5.5, AV. 5.7, total 5.6
Percentage move	IMT 7.5, AV. 25.9
Length of trade (weeks)	6

The profit-to-risk ratio of this trade was excellent at 5.6. In this example both the long and the short component in the portfolio produced good profits but that is not essential for success.

The examples used in this chapter only have one short and one long in the portfolio, however many variations of this are possible, depending on one's objectives and available speculative funds. The examples balance exposure between long and short components by equalising the maximum loss on each component, again variations are possible which equalise the exposure to the underlying. The overall purpose of the strategy is to take advantage of sector trends when the overall market is going sideways.

Strategy 7 – Early Bird

Introduction to the strategy

This strategy is for stocks. It is a long only strategy designed to catch the bottom of a down-trend, or a move from sideways to up. This is a high risk strategy which occasionally provides a big winner. It is high risk because down-trends are prone to merely pause and then continue on down; it may take several goes at probing for a bottom before we are successful.

Strategy methodology

The basic methodology of this strategy is:

1. overall market can be going down, sideways or up

2. the stock's sector displays momentum divergence

3. the stock displays momentum divergence

4. we receive a signal to enter a long trade

5. we determine how much capital to risk

6. we determine where our protective stop will be

7. we calculate trade size based on 5 and 6

8. then we go long

9. we trail our protective stop as the trade moves in our favour; we include a time stop if the trade fails to reach certain milestones

Advantages and disadvantages of the strategy

The main advantages of this strategy are:

- We can get into a new up-trend early and ride a large portion of it.

- Our trade size is a function of how much we are prepared to risk and where our stop will be.

- The time stop allows us to abort if the trade fails to reach certain milestones.

The main disadvantage of this strategy is that opportunities to trade it tend to come in bunches, nothing for a year or longer, then a whole series of opportunities.

Technical challenges of the strategy

The main technical challenges in implementing this strategy are:

1. what time frame to trade this strategy

2. how to define momentum divergence

3. how to define the signal to enter a long trade

4. how to determine how much capital to risk

5. how to determine where to put our protective stop

6. how to define the signal to exit

We will now look at answering these questions.

Solutions to the technical challenges of the strategy

1) What time frame to trade this strategy on

We will take trades off weekly charts, and expect trades to last from weeks to months.

2) How to define momentum divergence

We will use a 6 period momentum indicator over a three month period; we will define divergence as the momentum indicator having made its lowest low of the period at least two weeks before the point where price makes its lowest low.

3) How to define the signal to enter a long trade

We will define the entry signal as price rising above the high of the last week.

4) How to determine how much capital to risk

For all the examples we will assume we have total speculative funds of £20,000, and we will risk 1% on each trade (i.e. £200).

> *Note*: This is a solution for traders who have mastered all the relevant techniques – less experienced traders should risk less than this (e.g. 0.25% or less).

5) How to determine where to put our protective stop

We will place our protective stop immediately below the low price used to determine momentum divergence.

6) How to define the signal to exit

We will adopt a patient solution, not trailing our protective stop until we have a profit of at least twice our initial risk; then we will trail our stop below the low of the previous two weeks. However, we will also impose a time limit for a new up-trend to emerge: if at the end of the tenth week in the trade it has never reached that point where the profit is at least twice our initial risk we will exit at the open the following week.

Example 1 – BAE

The next two charts show the set up for this trade.

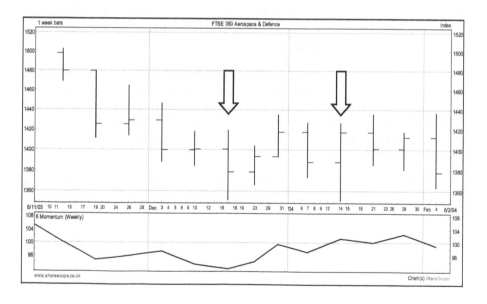

The Aerospace and Defence sector is displaying momentum divergence. At the second arrow price has made the lowest low in the three month period (only just, but that is OK). At that point the momentum indicator has made its lowest low of the period at least two weeks earlier, at the first arrow.

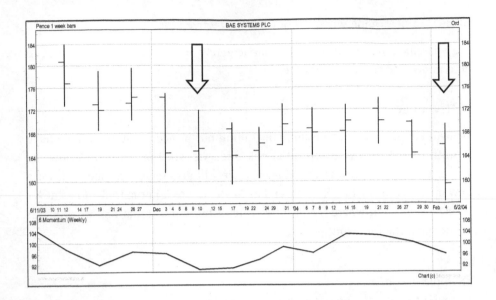

The stock BAE Systems PLC is displaying momentum divergence. At the second arrow price has made the lowest low in the three month period. At that point the momentum indicator has made its lowest low of the period at least two weeks earlier, at the first arrow.

We will enter long if price exceeds the high of the last week, with a stop below the low of the period. Our entry price will be 169.75p, with a stop at 156.5p.

Bets in BAE Systems are priced in pounds per point (penny), so we will bet £15 per point. Our risk will be £198.75, in line with our predetermined maximum risk per trade (169.75 – 156.5 times 15).

We set all of this up on our spread betting platform with a buy stop to enter at 169.75, £15 per point, and a contingent order to place a protective stop if filled.

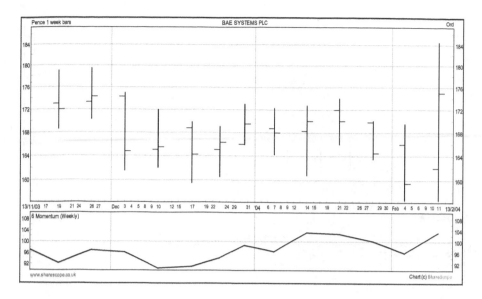

During the week we were filled at 169.75, and our protective stop has been placed automatically at 156.5. According to the rules of this strategy we will leave the protective stop there until price hits the level where we have achieved a profit of twice our risk, which is at 196.25 (169.75 plus (169.75 – 156.5 times 2)).

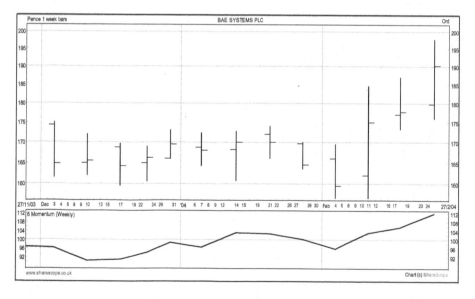

This week we have reached that 196.25 level, so now we move our protective stop below the low of the last two weeks, to 173.0, thereby locking in a small profit of £48.75 (173 – 169.75 times 15).

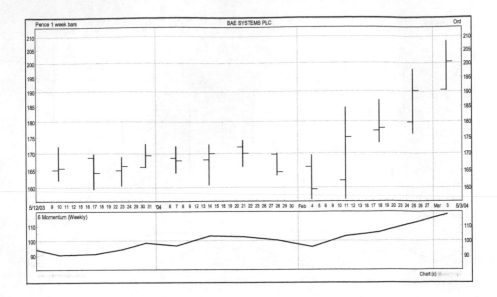

We move our stop again to below the low of the last two weeks, to 175.75, locking in a profit of £90.

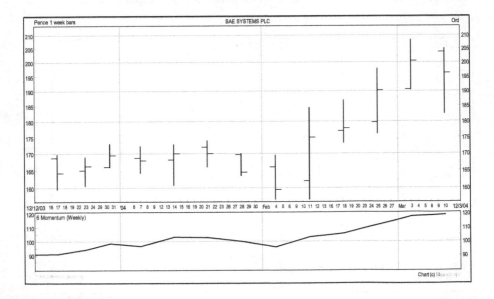

We move our stop again to below the low of the last two weeks, to 182.25, locking in a profit of £187.50.

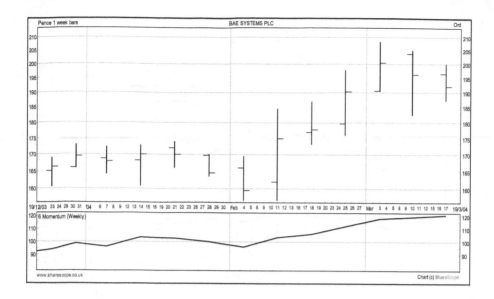

The low of the last two weeks has not changed this week, so the stop stays at the same level.

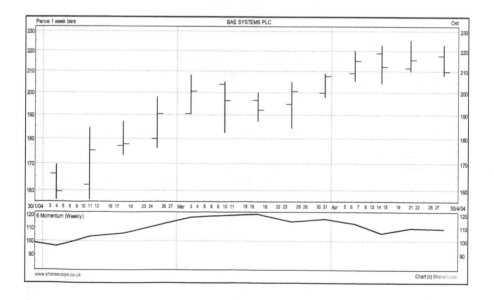

Another six weeks on, and we have been trailing our stop regularly upwards, to just below the low of the last two weeks. It is now at 207.75, locking in a profit of £570.

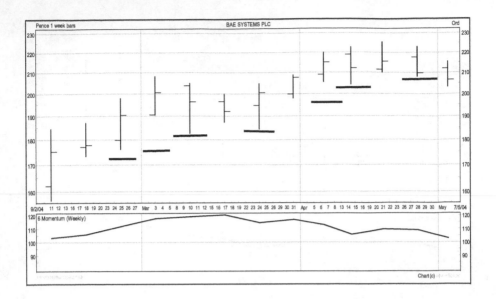

This week our stop was hit, we are out of the trade. The chart shows how we have trailed the stop through the latter stages of the trade. (The thick lines under the bars show when a stop was moved).

Trade summary

Field	Value
Instrument	BAE Systems
Long / short	Long
Entry	169.75
£s per point	15
Protective stop	156.5
Exit	207.75
Risk (£s)	198.75
Risk as a % of trading capital	1.0
Profit (£s)	570
Profit-to-risk ratio	2.9
Percentage move	22.4
Length of trade (weeks)	13

A solid trade, with a reward-to-risk ratio of 2.9.

An alterative approach to this type of strategy is to just bag a profit two times the risk as soon as it is achieved. We got to that point in only the third week of the trade, and we have spent the remaining ten weeks merely increasing the reward-to-risk ratio from 2.0 to 2.9. As always, there are trade-offs. Staying in longer, following our formulated rules, gave us a shot at a much bigger winner, even though on this occasion it didn't materialise.

Example 2 – BHP Billiton
The next two charts show the set up for this trade.

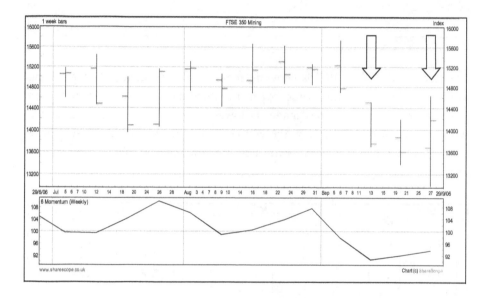

The Mining sector is showing momentum divergence. At the second arrow price has made the lowest low in the three month period. At that point the momentum indicator has made its lowest low of the period at least two weeks earlier, at the first arrow.

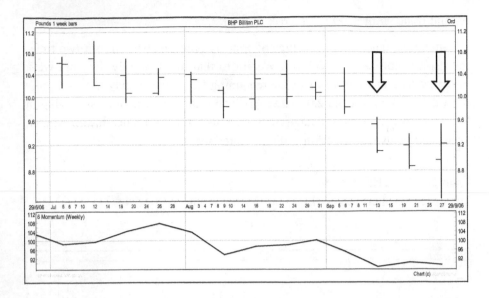

The stock BHP Billiton PLC is showing momentum divergence. At the second arrow price has made the lowest low in the three month period. At that point the momentum indicator has made its lowest low of the period at least two weeks earlier, at the first arrow. We will enter a long trade if price rises above the high of the previous week, with a stop below the low of the three month period.

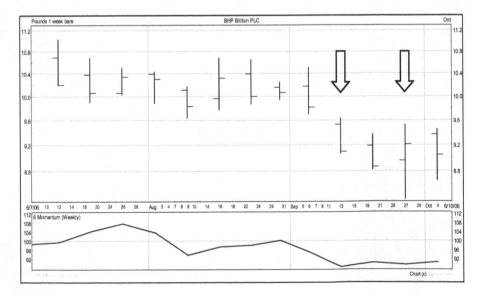

Momentum divergence is still valid a week later, but price failed to rise above the high of the week.

We will enter a long trade is price rises above the high of this latest week, with a stop below the low of the three month period. Our entry price will be 945.25, and our stop will be at 838.75.

Bets in BHP Billiton are priced in pounds per point (penny). We will bet £2 per point. Our risk will be £213, just acceptable regarding our predetermined maximum risk per trade. We placed our orders on the spread betting platform in advance of the next week's market open. We use a stop order for entry, and a contingent order to place our protective stop if our entry order is triggered.

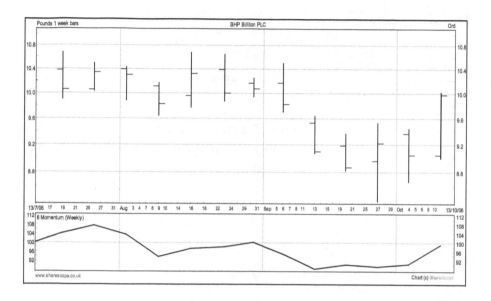

Price rose during the week above the high of the previous week, and the spread betting platform automatically entered us long at 945.25 with a stop at 838.75. We will leave our stop at 838.75 until price hits a point where we will have a profit twice our initial risk. That point is 1158.25 (945.25 plus (945.25 – 838.75 times 2)).

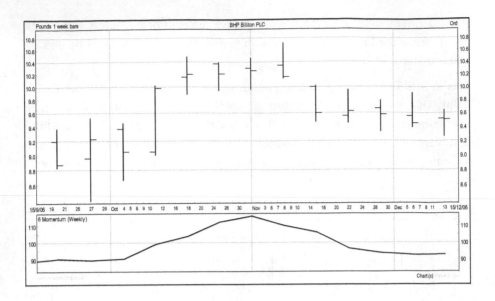

We are at the end of the tenth week of the trade, but price has never got to that 1158.25 level. Time to abort and look for other opportunities elsewhere. We will exit when the markets open next week.

Our exit price is 945.0p.

Trade summary

Field	Value
Instrument	BHP Billiton PLC
Long / short	Long
Entry	945.25
£s per point	2
Protective stop	838.75
Exit	945.0
Risk (£s)	213
Risk as a % of trading capital	1.1
Loss (£s)	0.50
Loss to risk ratio	0.0
Percentage move	0.0
Length of trade (weeks)	10

We have ended up with a scratched trade, a negligible loss after ten weeks. The maximum paper profit we had on the trade was £251.50, but that has obviously gone, as we pursued the potential for a bigger profit.

Once again, a trade-off in the design of the strategy: we hold out for profit twice our risk before we move our protective stop. We could, if we wanted, change the whole structure of the strategy if we changed the exit rules.

Example 3 - ICAP

The next two charts show the set up for this trade.

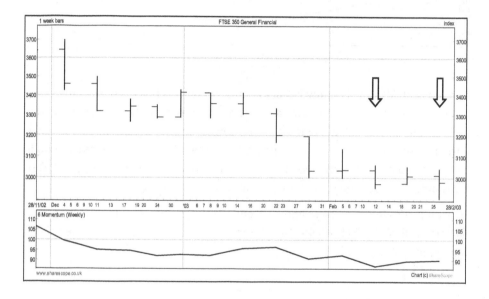

The General Financial sector is showing momentum divergence. At the second arrow price has made the lowest low in the three month period. At that point the momentum indicator has made its lowest low of the period at least two weeks earlier, at the first arrow.

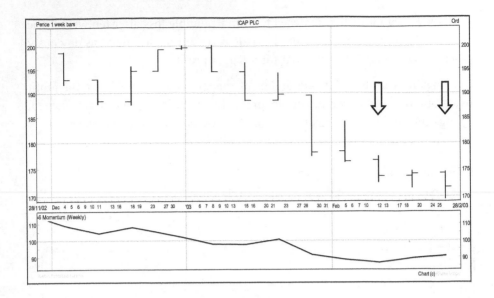

The stock ICAP PLC is showing momentum divergence. At the second arrow price has made the lowest low in the three month period. At that point the momentum indicator has made its lowest low of the period at least two weeks earlier, at the first arrow. We will enter a long trade if price rises above the high of the previous week, with a stop below the low of the three month period. Our entry price will be 174.75p, and our stop will be at 169.25p.

Bets on ICAP are priced in pounds per point (penny). We will bet £36 per point. Our risk will be £198 (174.75 – 169.25 times 36), in line with our predetermined maximum risk per trade.

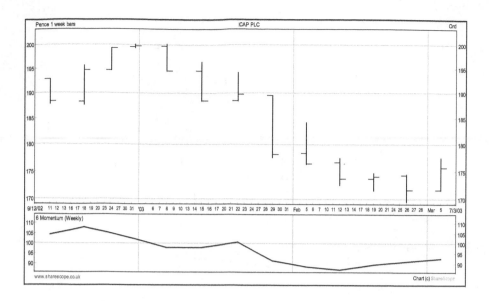

During the week price rose above the high of the previous week, and the spread betting platform automatically put us in a long trade at 174.75, with a protective stop at 169.25.

We will leave that stop in place until a price level is hit at which we have a profit of twice our risk. That level is 185.75 (174.75 plus (174.75 – 169.25 times 2).

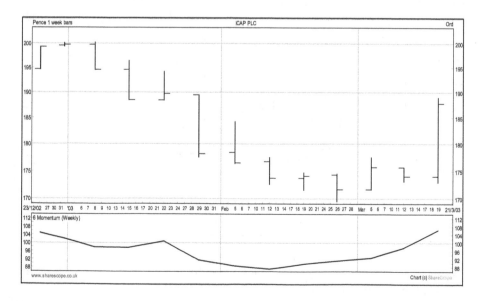

Now price has hit the 185.75 level we trail a stop below the low of the last two weeks. We move our stop to 172.75, limiting our risk on the trade now to £72.

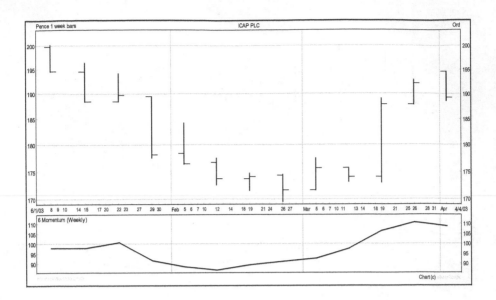

We move our stop again to below the low of the last two weeks, to 187.5, locking in a profit of £459.

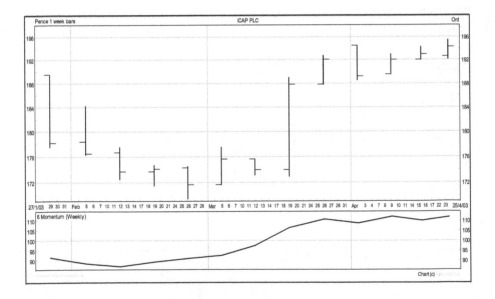

We have moved our stop several times since the previous chart, it is now at 191.75, locking in a profit of £612.

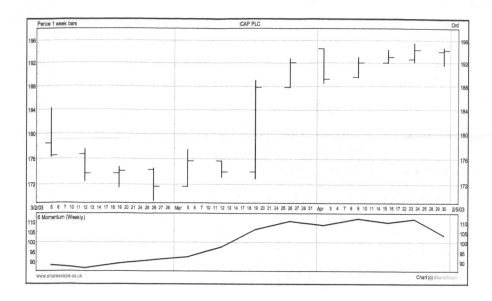

Our stop was hit in the week, we are out of the trade.

Trade summary

Field	Value
Instrument	ICAP PLC
Long / short	Long
Entry	174.75
£s per point	36
Protective stop	169.25
Exit	191.75
Risk (£s)	198
Risk as a % of trading capital	1.0
Profit (£s)	612
Profit-to-risk ratio	3.1
Percentage move	9.7
Length of trade (weeks)	9

A solid trade, with a reward-to-risk ratio of 3.1.

As it happens during the course of the trade the moving average configuration changed from sideways to up-trend mode. Just because the strategy has us exiting right now it does not mean we will be denied an opportunity to profit from that up-trend later.

Each strategy has its purpose.

This strategy has enabled us to get on board at the very start of a new up-trend and ride it for a while. To get back on board the up-trend at a suitable moment in the future we have other strategies.

Which, hopefully, as we reach the conclusion of Part Two, you know already!

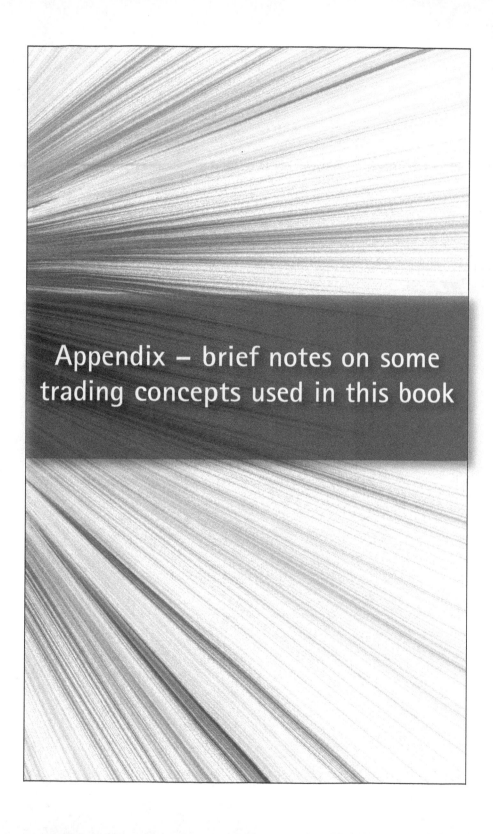

Appendix – brief notes on some
trading concepts used in this book

The topics covered in this appendix are:

1. Exit methodology

2. Bet size

3. Shorting

4. Diversification

5. Drawdown

Exit methodology

Successful traders tend to spend as much time on trade exit methodology as entry methodology. In other words: *when do you get out?*

Many of the strategies in this book use a trailing stop based around the low or the high of the previous two weeks. This type of exit methodology is intended to help run winners while actively managing the risk of a trade.

But it is only one type of exit methodology and if you already have alternative techniques which you like, then go ahead and change the strategy methodology to reflect this.

One alternative technique that I like – both for stop placement and bet size determination – is *Average True Range.* Briefly, Average True Range looks at the difference between the high and the low of each period (the number of periods determined by the user), and averages them. Some traders and investors use various multiples of Average True Range away from, say, the latest close to set stops and calculate bet size. A great technique, and if you have already mastered it, you may prefer to use it rather than the two period high or low used in this book.

Bet size

Some experts deem bet size to be one of the most important factors in a trading strategy. Dr Van Tharp has recently published an entire book on this subject called *Van Tharp's Definitive Guide to Position Sizing – How to Evaluate your System and Use Position Sizing to Meet your Objectives* (2008) which I commend to readers.

Bet size needs to be matched to an individual's objectives and risk preferences. In this book we use a default bet size of 1% of capital for illustrative purposes, but for many traders this will not be the right figure.

Interestingly, for many of the traders attending my seminars on spread betting bet size is an area they have got badly wrong in the past. We find that many of them have been betting way too much per bet. Bet size strategy is a key ingredient which separates the winners from the losers.

So, do get back to me with messages like: "I found Strategy X really interesting, but I have found it is better for me to make the following amendments to it..."!

The best place to discuss this is the forum on the website I edit:

www.spreadbettingcentral.co.uk

Shorting

Shorting is a key component in several of the strategies and illustrated in many of the examples. It is shorting which enables us to take advantage of downward price movement as well as upward.

One simple way of looking at it is this. When going *long* of a stock we make a purchase of the stock first, then sell it later, hoping that between the first event and the second event the price of the stock rises. When going *short* of a stock we make the sale of the stock first, then buy it later, hoping that between the first event and the second event the price of the stock falls. There are a number of procedural issues which can make this quite complicated to implement in a stockbroking account. But one of the great advantages of spread betting as a trading tool is that it is as straightforward to go short with it as it is to go long. One makes a *down* bet rather than an *up* bet.

If you have never shorted before you can see how it works in the examples in this book. Just bear in mind that the basic concept is very simple, particularly when spread betting is used to implement it: one is betting that prices will go down rather than up.

Diversification

Another significant advantage of spread betting is that it enables investors to diversify by easily gaining exposure to asset classes other than stocks. In addition to being able to place bets on indices as well as individual stocks, one can also place bets on currencies, commodities and interest rate products. During 2008 many investors sat and watched their stock portfolios fall in value. They could have used spread betting to go short during this period. But also there were some great moves in currencies and commodities. For instance

Sterling Dollar went from over 2 to below 1.50. Oil soared to over $140 then fell back down to below $50. The *spread betting investor* aims to take advantage of such moves.

Drawdown

When operating an investment strategy it is almost certain that the results will contain a mixture of winners and losers. The slope of the equity curve produced by the strategy is usually jagged rather than smooth. The periods when equity is falling are called *drawdowns*.

There are various ways to measure drawdown. One commonly used method is to measure how much equity dips from peak to trough. Investors' tolerance of drawdown varies, and this is one of many reasons why a strategy that is effective for one person might not be suitable for another.

Index

currency pairs 54-59, 105-113, 142-146, 148-153, 154-155

D

Diaego charts 165, 167-168, 175
divergence 47, 185-198
Dollar Yen charts 105-113, 154-155
drawdown 23, 24, 207

E

edge 16, 17, 30
Euro Dollar charts 54-59, 148-153
exit points xii, 8, 47, 205
      - predetermine 18
      - techniques 18
      - worked examples 31-202
experience, importance of 29

F

Financial Spread Betting Handbook, The ix, xii, 30
Fixed Line Telecommunications Index chart 101
flowing up-trend 40
fundamental analysis 25
Futures 24

G

Galiform charts 131-135
gambling xix, 23
General Financial sector chart 197

H

Household Goods Index chart 126

I

ICAP 197-201
Imperial Tobacco Group charts 178-180
individual, each investor as xiii, 33, 205

K

L

M

O

P

R

S

T

W

V